BEDTIME
SNACKS
~ for the ~
SOUL
Meditations to
Sweeten Your Dreams

Other Books by This Author

BEDTIME SNACKS

for the

SOUL

Meditations to Sweeten Your Dreams

DIANE M. KOMP, M.D.

ZondervanPublishingHouse

Grand Rapids, Michigan

A Division of HarperCollinsPublishers

Bedtime Snacks for the Soul
Copyright © 2000 by Diane M. Komp

Requests for information should be addressed to:

⛪ ZondervanPublishingHouse
Grand Rapids, Michigan 49530

Library of Congress Cataloging-in-Publication Data

Komp, Diane M.
    Bedtime snacks for the soul : meditations to sweeten your dreams / Diane M. Komp.
      p. cm.
    Includes bibliographical references.
    ISBN 0-310-23562-6 (hardcover)
    1. Meditations. 2. Devotional calendars. I. Title.
BV4811.K66 2000
242'.2 — dc21   00-043648
                                                                   CIP

Interior design by Sue Vandenberg Koppenol

Printed in the United States of America

00 01 02 03 04 05 06 /❖ WZ/ 10 9 8 7 6 5 4 3 2 1

*May God ever dress our days in peace
and starlight order.*
From an ancient vesper hymn

CONTENTS

Week 6:
SILENT NIGHT

Week 7:
RISEN WITH HEALING IN HIS WINGS

PREFACE

Yawn.
Stretch.
Ready for bed?
Stop right there!

Before you turn in tonight, I have an important question for you. If you had to choose a single word to describe your relationship with God when you go to bed at night, what one word would that be? Fill in the blank in this sentence for me: "At bedtime my spiritual life is _____."

Well, what word did you choose?

I've been asking lots of folks this question lately and am absolutely amazed at some of the words they pick. More often than not these friends in faith express an element of defeat when they talk about their bedtime spirituality. Here are some words they select to indicate their level of frustration:

At bedtime my spiritual life is

    shot
    blank
    zip
    inconsistent
    frustrating
    under siege
    running on empty
    dry
    flat-line

For busy people, the "peace and starlight order" of the vesper hymn seems like an exquisite but inaccessible dream. And yet, we all long for a solid sense of God's benediction on our days—don't we?

The barriers that keep us from that goal are quite simple. When we retire from the day, *we don't retire from the problems of our day.* We don't empty the pockets of our mind of the things that hamper refreshing sleep. At night we hold on to our insoluble daytime aggravations while we do a two-step shuffle from *thinking* about our problems to *feeling* their full weight upon our shoulders.

Morning is far different, I believe. I may not feel like getting out of bed at dawn, but eventually logic wins out over my feelings. If I were to stay nestled under a cozy quilt rather than hit the shower, I could lose my job. That dumb I'm not, so splash-me-awake reason prevails over snuggle-down-under feelings.

Most of us can make that transition to thinking in the morning, but it's hard to reason at night when we are running on empty. But if we are running on empty, how can we get our spiritual tanks refilled? I believe we can benefit from those who have a positive view of the same sack-time circumstances. Contrast these answers with the previous defeated nighttime vignettes:

At bedtime my spiritual life is

> focused
> quiet
> calming
> nourishing
> fullest
> trusting
> renewed
> alive
> contemplative

What a difference a choice of words can make! Since I suspect I am more a flat-liner than a contemplative myself, I want to know the secrets of those who have abundantly encountered God in their last moments before sleep. These clues from the "focused" became the backbone for this bedtime devotional book.

I've chosen seven different forms in which words and pictures can come together to tell a holy bedtime story: dreams, prayers, vesper hymns, psalms, poems, canticles, and power words. This may sound like an odd thing for a professor to say, but I chose selections that will not stimulate profound thinking. Am I offering you quiet time lite? No, not really. I think of these spiritual bedtime snacks as quiet time right—the right-size meal for this time of the day.

We are supposed to fall asleep when we go to bed, not stay awake to solve the problems of the universe. The less weighty our evening meals, the easier our digestion, and the more prepared are our bodies for sleep. I think the same is true of our nighttime devotions. But I do have a little work for you to do.

Some of us grew up memorizing Bible verses, but few of us actively continued this practice into our adult lives. Even those of us who want to can hardly find the time to add fresh verses to our heart-hidden treasure. What about those last moments of the day when the rhythm of repetition might actually help us fall asleep? Here's my scheme.

For each evening, I've chosen a short comforting Bible verse that I'm sure you would like to know by heart. I tied one of these verses to each bedtime snack in a "sweet dreams tip." No, don't write the verses down! The lights will be off by the time you repeat them until you fall asleep.

So . . .

Turn off the TV.

Shut down your computer. (No checking e-mail in the middle of the night!)

Let the dog take you out for a short walk.

Extinguish the lights in the living room, kitchen, study—everywhere in the house you work.

Take off your shoes.

Thank the dog for bringing your slippers.

Now, get ready for bed.

If you don't feel quite sleepy yet . . .

Soak in a hot bubble bath.

Amble toward your bedroom.

Turn on a soft light.

Look around your bedroom for things that remind you of sleep.

Slip under the covers.

Breathe easy, in and out.

In.

Out.

In.

Now you can begin to sweeten your dreams.

Diane M. Komp, M.D.
Guilford, Connecticut

1
MIDDLE-OF-THE-NIGHT MIRACLES

Dreams do not unlock the secrets of the universe nor inspire the dreamer to pen a poem or paint a great work of art. But they do provide wisdom and discernment for how to handle difficult circumstances.

Ann Spangler, *Dreams and Miracles*, adapted

Day 1:

THE INTERPRETED DREAM

I have heard it said of you that when you hear a dream you can interpret it.
Genesis 41:15

Twelve-year-old Aldo* was sitting on the examining table in my office, unbuttoning his shirt, stripping for medical action.

"Aldo, tell the dottora about your dreama."

"Nah, Ma," Aldo shook his head. The boy was blushing crimson red, his rosy cheeks accentuating his cherubic altar-boy demeanor.

"Aldo, tell the dottora about your dreama!"

Mamma Leone's tone was getting more insistent. The woman was on a mission. I put down my stethoscope and glanced over at her son. In turn, Aldo looked up at the ceiling, averting his eyes from mine.

"You tell her, Ma," Aldo grinned. And she did.

"Dottora, my Aldo, he had a dreama."

Thus a Sicilian mamma started a lesson about dreams far more important than anything I had learned about them in medical school.

---

* To honor privacy, I've changed some names and minor details in these stories.

When I was a child of Aldo's age, I learned about biblical dreams with special meaning. Jacob saw a ladder filled with angels. Joseph saw sheaves of grain in a field. King Nebuchadnezzar couldn't remember his dream, and that bothered him a lot. Fascinating stories, but that was long before I heard of Sigmund Freud and his ideas about dream interpretation.

From where my classmates and I sat in medical school, it seemed that Freudian dream symbols could be placed into one of the following three interpretative categories: sex, sex, or sex. With the exception of a handful of our cronies who wanted to be psychiatrists, it is safe to say that most of us thought this sort of monotonous dream interpretation stretched credulity.

As I sat in class and thought about this, I never remembered having any dreams myself. Thus I dismissed the notion that dreams might have any significance. This was around the same time I dismissed the Christian faith in which I had been nurtured—a sad non-coincidence, typical of modern medical education. But once Mamma Leone started telling the tale of her Aldo's dreama, there was no way to stop her.

Whatever I believed or disbelieved, my only option was to listen to Mamma Leone. Although Aldo had seemed reluctant to tell me the dream himself, out of the corner of my eye I spied a smile on his face as we listened to his mamma weave her colorful narrative.

"Dottora, in this dreama my Aldo he had, dottora, God, he come into the rooma where my Aldo he was. And dottora, God, he put his hand on my Aldo's head. And dottora, when God he touched my Aldo, dottora, electricity she runa down the arma."

From the top of her shoulders to the tips of her fingers, Mamma Leone stroked her own arms to illustrate what she meant. Goose bumps rose on her flesh at the touch of her own fingers. You would have thought that she had been there with Aldo in his dreama.

"Dottora," Mamma Leone asked me, "the dreama, what she meana?"

Suddenly I recalled King Nebuchadnezzar asking young Daniel the very same question. What did the king's dream mean? And I remembered the penalty Daniel faced if the king didn't like his interpretation. In that same moment it occurred to me that there isn't a tremendous difference between a Babylonian king who wants to hear that he's the greatest king in the history of the world and a Sicilian mamma who wants to hear that her son has been healed of leukemia and doesn't need any more chemotherapy.

Aldo's smile curved into a grin as he watched me intently, wondering how—or if—I'd escape the lion's den his mamma was preparing for me.

"Aldo!" I said, turning away from Mamma and placing my hands on the youngster's shoulders. "Aldo, isn't that a wonderful dream?"

Mamma eyed me suspiciously. Intently. Hopefully.

"Aldo, how wonderful that God knows about the medicine vincristine! God wanted you to know that your medicine is part of his plan for you."

Aldo beamed brightly, and Mamma cast me a look as if to say, "You wiggled out of it this time, but you justa waita for the nexta timea!"

Both Aldo and Mamma recalled that I had told them about a peculiar side effect of vincristine, part of his chemotherapy. Vincristine causes what, in medical lingo, we call "paresthesia." In lay terms you could say that means that electricity, she runa down your arma.

Twenty years have passed since Aldo's wonderful dream. Praise God, he's a healthy adult today, as are many children we treated with vincristine. Many of them have been touched in their spirits as well as in their bodies, like this young man. Mamma was touched in her spirit the day Aldo told her his dream. And so was I the day they shared Aldo's dream with me.

That touch in our spirit is the touch we all need the most. At a bare minimum, Aldo's dream expressed a child's integration of two vital aspects of his life—his health and his spiritual nature. At a happy maximum, the dream recorded God's healing visit to touch a frightened child. Either interpretation is a powerful lesson for a doctor, a mamma, and a fearful little boy. This is a message about dreams that Sigmund Freud was not competent to deliver.

Before I met Aldo and Mamma, I thought of medicine and faith as rivals for my mind. No one in medical school ever told me I would meet patients who longed to be touched by a living God. Surely God was in that high-tech hospital and I hadn't even known it!

Since Aldo came into my life, I've learned I am a dreamer too. In recent years I've looked into my dreams and noted that I long to be touched by God as well. Surely God was in my own life all those many years and I never even knew it!

 Do you remember a dream in which God seemed to come and touch you? As you fall asleep tonight, recreate the images of that dream as you repeat, "Surely the LORD is in this place—and I did not know it" (Genesis 28:16 NRSV).

Day 2:
A Child's Prayer*

Nothing is so beautiful as a child going to sleep while he is saying his prayers, says God. I tell you nothing is so beautiful in the world.

Charles Péguy, *Basic Verities*

If Aldo taught me to listen to children when they talk about their dreams, Scotty taught me to pay strict attention to what children have to say about their prayers. I was making rounds one day when Scotty's mother told him that, in addition to being a doctor, I write books.

"What do you write about?" he asked me. I sat down on the edge of Scotty's bed to make us both comfortable.

"Well," I told him, "a long time ago I figured out that I didn't have all the answers to life's most important questions. I learned that when I listen to kids—kids like you—I get more sensible answers than I hear from most adults. So I listen to children's stories and I write them down. I'm just the secretary."

Scotty grinned, pleased that I seemed to know my place in life. And he seemed prepared to make sure that I stayed in place.

"You know," he said, warming up his story, "not everything in science is true. And not everything in religion either."

What a spontaneous statement to come from a thirteen-year-old lad who didn't know anything about me except that I am a doctor who writes books! I could imagine adult patients riddled with doubts about science and doubts about faith, but would they even think to give words to their thoughts? I decided to explore Scotty's scientific reservations first.

"What is it in science that you have difficulty believing?" I asked him.

"Well, take the Big Bang theory, for instance," he replied.

"Okay," I said. "What's your problem with the Big Bang theory?"

"They say that the world came about by accident, but when I look at the world and everything in it, I see a design and a plan. I could be wrong, but I doubt it."

Scotty folded his arms across his chest, firming up his position. With science put squarely in its place, we moved on to his other area of doubt.

"What is it about religion that you have trouble believing?" I asked him.

"Well, take David and Goliath, for instance."

David and Goliath? *David and Goliath?* The little kids' friends? I had never in my life met a child who had difficulty with David and Goliath!

"What, pray tell, is your problem with David and Goliath?" I asked him.

"Well, they say that Goliath was eight foot four inches tall, and there is nobody that tall," Scotty said firmly.

"I've seen some pretty tall basketball players in my time," I countered.

"Not that tall," he insisted.

I was losing the argument, so I got medical.

"There's this pituitary condition where you keep making more and more growth hormone, and you keep growing and growing and growing."

"Not that tall," Scotty said. His arms recrossed his breast to hold his position tight. But then he became very quiet.

"You know," he said softly, "it's not the details that matter. It's the moral of the story."

I was speechless, and so was his mother, who was standing by the bedside wondering all this time, *Is this* my *son talking?*

I thought about this boy, immersed in the terrifying world of high-tech medicine. He was in my hospital because his cancer had returned with a vengeance. And then I thought about David and Goliath. Just what was the moral of these stories, young Scotty's and young David's?

Both stories are tales of lads who would prevail against something that was *unbelievably big*. As big as Goliath. As big as death. But Scotty wasn't finished with me yet.

"Do you pray?" he asked me.

Patients don't often ask their doctors this question!

"Yes, I do. Do you pray?" I threw back at him.

"Every night," he retorted.

"Now that really interests me," I said. "And I need to learn a lot about prayer. Perhaps if you told me what you know about prayer, I might learn something helpful. Tell me how you pray."

"I start by saying a prayer," Scotty said, and started reciting a child's prayer from rote memory: "NowIlaymedowntosleep." But then he looked up, as if he could see the words he was saying in front of his eyes, with the prayer written on a ticker-tape. His words slowed down to match his measured breaths. "Now I lay me down to sleep. I pray the Lord my soul to keep."

As he looked up at those invisible but powerfully present words, Scotty started nodding as if he agreed with himself, agreed with what he had just read. "If I should die before I wake" (his nodding became more vigorous) "I pray the Lord my soul to take." He was pleased with his words. "And then I pray for everyone I know."

"I tell you what, Scotty," I said. "I'll pray for you if you'll pray for me."

The boy smiled softly, and then he said, "I've already been praying for you. Every night I pray for all the doctors and nurses on the team."

After I left his hospital room, Scotty asked Rachel, one of his nurses, "Do you think Dr. Komp will ever write about me?" Rachel's answer has come true in this book: "You had better believe it!" You had better believe it, too. The moral of Scotty's story is meant to be shared.

Prayer is how we agree with God's design and plan for our lives. Prayer is how we discern the moral to our stories. In the face of whatever is unbelievably big in our lives tonight, we can believe that the Creator of the universe is thinking about you and thinking about me.

Recall a prayer from your childhood that made you feel you were part of God's design and plan as you "seek him that made the Pleiades and Orion, that turneth deep darkness into the morning, and darkeneth the day into night" (Amos 5:8 BCP).

*Portions of "A Child's Prayer" were first published in Spiro, Curnan, and Wandel, eds., *Facing Death*, © Yale University Press. Reprinted with permission.

Day 3:

O THE DEEP, DEEP LOVE OF JESUS

When you play songs, you can bring
back people's memories of when they
fell in love. That's where the power lies.
John Berendt, *Midnight in the*
Garden of Good and Evil

One of my favorite types of summer worship services is singing lots of congregation-picked hymns instead of hearing a sermon. Some of the shyest members of a church family are drawn out by this type of event. A pastor can learn more about the spiritual lives of the members on this one Sunday than during the entire rest of the year. But you can't just pick a hymn. You have to tell why it's your favorite.

One of the highlights I remember from such a service came from an elderly saint whose choice was the last hymn we would sing that particular Sunday. Time was running short when the pastor asked her to choose two of its five verses to conclude the service.

"You're going to sing all of them!" she declared boldly. "You're going to sing them all at my funeral in a few years, so you might as well start practicing now!"

Well, in this book I get to pick all the hymns and you get to sing all the verses! If you know the tunes to these hymns, sing along softly. If you don't know the tunes, you have the privilege to focus on the words. I'm sure by the time you finish with my favorites, you'll be thinking about your own beloved vespers that can sing you to sleep when you have finished this book.

O THE DEEP, DEEP LOVE OF JESUS

O the deep, deep love of Jesus,
    vast, unmeasured, boundless, free!
Rolling as a mighty ocean
    in its fullness over me!
Underneath me, all around me,
    is the current of thy love
Leading onward, leading homeward
    to thy glorious rest above!

❧

O the deep, deep love of Jesus,
    spread his praise from shore to shore!
How he loveth, ever loveth,
    changeth never, nevermore!
How he watches o'er his loved ones,
    died to call them all his own;
How for them he intercedeth,
    watcheth o'er them from the throne!

❧

O the deep, deep love of Jesus,
    love of every love the best!

'Tis an ocean full of blessing,
    'tis a haven giving rest!
O the deep, deep love of Jesus,
    'tis a heaven of heavens to me;
And it lifts me up to glory,
    for it lifts me up to thee!

Samuel Trevor Francis

 Imagine the depth of Jesus' love for you as you repeat, "I am convinced that neither death, nor life, nor angels, nor rulers, nor things present, nor things to come, nor powers, nor height, nor depth, nor anything else in all creation, will be able to separate us from the love of God in Christ Jesus our Lord" (Romans 8:38–39 NRSV).

Day 4:

MOTHER IS A POWER WORD

Don't let our dreams fade into fantasies.
We want our children to dream, too.
Linda Ann Olson, *New Psalms*
for New Moms

Some of us need to dream more. Some of us even need to dream while we are awake. For Helen, investing herself in a godly daydream was a step forward in healing.

Helen was in an isolation room on a bone marrow transplant unit when I first met her. Her eighteen-month-old baby, Kaitlin, peeked over a baby gate that separated her from her mom. At this point Helen was so weakened by her treatment that a baby's kiss could kill her. She told me the story of her life.

Before Kaitlin came along, Helen had been a successful artist. The birth of this beautiful child had fulfilled her first godly dream. Since then Helen had been through so much. First there was chemotherapy for leukemia. Then a bone marrow transplant. But the bone marrow graft was sluggish in setting up shop, and a viral infection was threatening to do it in. I asked Helen how she had coped with it all. She sat back and smiled as she told me.

While the chemo was running, Helen had imagined that she was far above the world, sharing a magic carpet ride with Mary, the mother of Jesus. Just two moms out for the day, looking down at the world, checking up on what was going on. Everywhere they went in her imagination, Helen said, they had seen groups of children, playing, laughing. She and Mary had smiled at each other.

Then Helen's face turned dark. She sat up and fixed me with an almost angry glare. "All I ever wanted to be was a mother!" she cried.

She had been there at Kaitlin's birth and at her christening. She glanced over at her little girl, separated from her by the baby gate. Helen wanted more.

She wanted to see Kaitlin grow up, to take her to school, to guide her into womanhood, to be there on her wedding day. That was Helen's greatest fear: that she wouldn't be there for those wonderful days. That she wouldn't live to be Kaitlin's mom. But wasn't that her greatest hope as well? To see her little girl grow up! To take her to school! To guide her into womanhood! To be there on her wedding day! All those moments a mother dreams about.

I looked at Helen and saw the fear in her eyes. But I saw hope there as well. *"Mother,"* I said, "is a power word."

"Yes!" Helen cried. "Yes, it is! *Mother* is a power word!"

That was the day Helen started to heal. A few weeks later she was home with her family, living out the first steps of her godly daydream.

One of the good things about daydreams is that we have control over how they evolve. We can make choices. We can look over the world and notice the things that really matter. We can infuse our daydreams with hope. We can choose hope instead of fear. We can flip over our fears and find our power words.

Think about something you're afraid of. Now flip it over to find the hope that is rightfully yours as you repeat, "His divine power has given us everything we need for life and godliness" (2 Peter 1:3).

Day 5:

A SIMPLE SONG

Sing God a simple song . . .
Make it up as you go along.
Leonard Bernstein and Steven Schwartz,
"A Simple Song"

As a child I learned many psalms by heart. The genius of these simple songs is that even a child could understand what they mean. Unfortunately, adult human nature has something against simplicity. Somehow we don't feel sophisticated enough unless we can make a simple concept as complicated as we possibly can.

In my field—medicine—we doctors are notorious for using language our patients can hardly understand. Theologians have a way of doing the same thing when they're talking to each other. They speak almost a private spiritual dialect that only other academics understand, and then they forget who they're talking to when they climb in the pulpit. I had to learn to simplify my medical language to help my patients understand their own health. Ironically, I sometimes forget to simplify my theological language when I'm talking about matters of faith.

An inner-city family in our practice came to faith in Christ after their son became ill with leukemia. Wanting them to know that I shared that experience, I loaned them a book I had written, *A Window to Heaven*, that tells that story. A few days later one of my partners visited them in the ward and found them reading my book. Jack was grinning when he came back to our office and said, "You're going to get yourself out of this one! They wanted me to explain what an 'ersatz-existentialist' is."

A young friend of mine recently gave me excellent advice about my writing: K.I.S.S.—"Keep It Simple, Sweetheart." In this regard, the book of Psalms is simply great literature. Rather than speak in million-dollar words, the psalmists offer us priceless images and emotions that we recognize as our own. Nothing "ersatz" here. Psalm 96 is a marvelous song that is simply wonderful.

Psalm 96

Sing to the LORD a new song;
    sing to the LORD, all the earth.
Sing to the LORD, praise his name;
    proclaim his salvation day after day.
Declare his glory among the nations,
    his marvelous deeds among all peoples.

◦∽◦

For great is the LORD and most worthy of praise;
    he is to be feared above all gods.
For all the gods of the nations are idols,
    but the LORD made the heavens.
Splendor and majesty are before him;
    strength and glory are in his sanctuary.

◦∽◦

Ascribe to the LORD, O families of nations,
    ascribe to the LORD glory and strength.

Ascribe to the LORD the glory due his name;
    bring an offering and come into his courts.
Worship the LORD in the splendor of his holiness;
    tremble before him, all the earth.

Say among the nations, "The LORD reigns."
    The world is firmly established, it cannot be moved;
    he will judge the peoples with equity.
Let the heavens rejoice, let the earth be glad;
    let the sea resound, and all that is in it;
    let the fields be jubilant, and everything in them.
Then all the trees of the forest will sing for joy;
    they will sing before the LORD, for he comes,
    he comes to judge the earth.
He will judge the world in righteousness
    and the peoples in his truth.

 Be blessed and find sleep with the simply true thought that you can "sing to the LORD a new song" (Psalm 96:1).

Day 6:

PIECES OF MY QUILT

The soul is dyed the color of its thoughts.
Marcus Aurelius

My friend Cindy McDowell is a very cozy person. Her church made a fine choice when they called her to direct their caring ministries. One of Cindy's mottoes is, "If something is worth doing, it's worth doing with a flare." That's exactly how she carries out her life and her whole ministry—with a flare. I thought you'd enjoy Cindy's talking quilt as you snuggle safely under your own tonight.

PIECES OF MY QUILT

If quilts could *talk*,
    I'd like to think I'd hear just what they'd say,
    "I'll hold you close within my folds and wipe your tears away.
    I'll keep you warm and give you strength to face another day."
If quilts could talk . . .

If quilts could *sing*,
    I'd like to think I'd recognize each tune,
    The lullaby or funeral dirge or wedding march in June.

Both sweet and haunting melodies I'd listen to them croon.
If quilts could sing . . .

❧

If quilts could *write,*
    I'd like to think I'd read the words they'd pen,
    Of life and love and motherhood, of mystery without end.
    And, oh, the drama they could share of everywhere they'd been
If quilts could write . . .

❧

If quilts could *pray,*
    I'd like to think I'd feel each heartfelt prayer
    Of thankfulness or great concern for those within their care;
    Petitions to a loving God—the One who's always there.
If quilts could pray . . .

❧

The quilt of my own life
    Finds voice to *talk, sing, write* and *pray,*
    As it weaves a hundred stories in its own eclectic way.
And with each stitch of grace and hope my legacy is built;
    All fragments finally made a whole . . .
        the *pieces of my quilt.*

Lucinda McDowell[1]

As you snuggle under your blankets tonight, think about God's plan for your life as the design of an elegant quilt. Consider yourself covered by that pattern as you repeat, "Do not conform any longer to the pattern of this world, but be transformed by the renewing of your mind. Then you will be able to test and approve what God's will is—his good, pleasing and perfect will" (Romans 12:2).

Day 7:

THE SONG OF MOSES

*By faith [Moses] persevered because
he saw him who is invisible.*

Hebrews 11:27

All of Scripture is God-breathed, but there are moments in the Bible right in the middle of straight prose that just take your breath away. In the Bible's "canticles," a prophet seems to break out into superinspired song phrased by matchless poetry. Moses, that "man of slow speech," was just such a chanticleer.

The occasion for the Song of Moses was the parting of the Red Sea, the safe passage of the children of Israel, and the drowning of the Egyptians who pursued the runaway slaves. I wonder if Moses ever tried to complain to God again about his oratorical skills after this experience?

When canticles are read publicly, the congregation usually divides to read the song antiphonally, that is, alternating phrases. If you're a couple sharing this devotional together tonight, alternate reading with each other, using the song's indentation as a guide. Many Christians add the "Gloria Patria" whenever a canticle is read or chanted, and I've added this familiar formula of faith as a benediction to our reading as well.

The Song of Moses (Cantemus Domino)

I will sing to the LORD,
    for he is highly exalted.
The horse and its rider
    he has hurled into the sea.
The LORD is my strength and my song;
    he has become my salvation.
He is my God, and I will praise him,
    my father's God, and I will exalt him.
The LORD is a warrior;
    the LORD is his name.
Pharaoh's chariots and his army
    he has hurled into the sea.
The best of Pharaoh's officers
    are drowned in the Red Sea.
The deep waters have covered them;
    they sank to the depths like a stone.

❧

Your right hand, O LORD,
    was majestic in power.
Your right hand, O LORD,
    shattered the enemy. . . .

❧

Who among the gods is like you, O LORD?
    Who is like you—
        majestic in holiness,
        awesome in glory,

working wonders?
You stretched out your right hand
   and the earth swallowed them.

❧

In your unfailing love you will lead
   the people you have redeemed.
In your strength you will guide them
   to your holy dwelling....

❧

You will bring them in and plant them
   on the mountain of your inheritance—
the place, O Lord, you made for your dwelling,
   the sanctuary, O Lord, your hands established.
The Lord will reign
   for ever and ever.

Exodus 15:1–6, 11–13, 17–18

*Glory be to the Father, and to the Son, and to the Holy Spirit:
As it was in the beginning, is now, and will be for ever. Amen.*

 *What has God saved you from? What does he still
need to save you from? Think of these things as you
repeat, "In your unfailing love you will lead the
people you have redeemed" (Exodus 15:13).*

2

MORE GROANS THAN WORDS

The best prayers have often more groans than words.

John Bunyan

Day 1:

THE RECURRENT DREAM

If during my sleep my mind wanders away into dreams, yet it only wanders upon holy ground.

Charles Spurgeon,
The Treasury of David

At the hospital, children became the reliable witnesses who brought me back to a new life of faith. Part of that new life became daily Bible study and prayer. That was when I learned that I too am a dreamer.

One morning I got up at my usual rising time of 5:30 A.M., read a chapter of Scripture, and lay back on my pillow to pray. Flush with the spiritual enthusiasm of a new believer, I prided myself that I could lie in bed praying without falling asleep. I bet you know where this story is leading—back to sleep.

While I was in the sort of shallow sleep where most dreams occur, I dreamed that I was at the office and screaming at a coworker. I was enraged. Unlike Aldo's beautiful dream, this was a nightmare. Here in this stupid dream, my anger was overflowing.

"Stupid"—that's right. I called the dream stupid. And ugly, just like the mood I was in when I woke up and realized that I had "fallen asleep on the job." That's exactly the way I described this incident later in the day to a Christian friend.

"And as if it weren't bad enough that I fell asleep on the job," I ranted, "the dream wasn't even a 'vision.' It was the same stupid dream I always have."

Hello? Same dream? But I thought I never dreamed!

After my dream about losing control and screaming, I smiled at the notion that God was sitting in heaven watching me and saying, "Girl, you still don't get it! How can I change the story line just enough that the main point stays the same but you finally pay attention?" This time God didn't change the story line. He simply changed my listening skills.

Recurrent dreams may not become apparent until after we've experienced the fifth, sixth, or seventh variation on the same theme. Through the process of telling my friend about that dream, I finally "got it." The anger I held in at work was brimming over and busting out at night. God chose his time (my quiet time) and his way (my dream) to show me that I had unfinished business that needed tending.

In that dream, I brought anger with me to work. But when Jesus sent his disciples out to do their business, he suggested a different approach (Luke 10:2–16). He didn't promise them an easy time of it. In fact, he told them they were like lambs sent out among wolves. But when they came to a new place, they were to say first as they entered, "Peace to this house." If they began their visit with peace and found responsive hearts in that house, they would be able to do their work and earn their wages.

It's not my basic nature to solve nasty problems at work with peace, so I've posted those words on the pinboard in my office:

"Peace to this house." But sometimes those four words get buried under a ton of yellow sticky Post-Its and I forget. Then, at night, the same dream comes back to remind me. The difference is that now I don't call the dream stupid.

Do you have a disturbing recurrent dream you don't understand? Try bringing peace to that dream house and see what happens in your life.

 Keep the images of a recurrent dream of your own in mind as you repeat, "When you enter a house, first say, 'Peace to this house!'" (Luke 10:5).

Day 2:

THE SPIRIT'S PRAYER

But there is the Holy Spirit! It's like a big thick blanket, like a down-filled comforter.
Gretchen Josephson, "Who To Pray To"

When Gretchen Josephson was born forty-six years ago, there was a medical term in use for babies with her condition—Mongoloid idiots. How cruel that word *idiot* sounds today when singled out to describe someone with Gretchen's spiritual sensitivity and her work history.

Gretchen's first job was as a bus girl at an elite downtown Denver tearoom. As early as junior high school, this young woman with Down's syndrome started to write poetry. Encouraged by one of her doctors, Gretchen's poetry found its way to print. My favorite poem in her collection *Bus Girl* is titled "Who To Pray To."[2]

In the poem, Gretchen talks about lying awake in the dark thinking, thinking, thinking. She muses whether to pray to the Father or to Jesus, and then she remembers that other member of the Trinity who, the apostle Paul tells us, intercedes for us with "groans that words cannot express" (Romans 8:26). Gretchen compares the Holy Spirit to a big thick blanket, a down-filled comforter. "Now I know who to pray to," she happily concludes.

I'm touched by Gretchen's trinitarian choice, because she has known her whole life what it is like to have thoughts and feelings that words cannot express. Perhaps this is why she feels so comfortable with the Holy Comforter. Like many other people with Down's syndrome, Gretchen's vocal tract has its problems. This young lady began speech therapy before she started kindergarten.

Gretchen has found many inexplicable things in her life to let the Holy Spirit groan about on her behalf. She muses, for example, that some of God's children are difficult at times. She notices that loneliness slowly sinks in when you know you are not perfect. She wonders what ministers and doctors and funeral directors have to do with the sting of death she has heard about in church.

Gretchen's concerns are the same as mine but, unlike this poet, I have faith in the powers of my tongue and brain to serve me unfailingly well. Some bright theologians have called people with Down's syndrome prophets in our midst. With or without their families' help, they find a relationship with God a natural thing. In comparison to them, it is the rest of us who are idiotic!

I'm so glad that Gretchen wrote her poems, especially the one about the Holy Spirit. I need fewer of my own words in prayer, and more of the Spirit of God to groan my concerns to the Father.

 Don't worry about finding the perfect words for your final prayer tonight. Fall asleep remembering to "pray in the Spirit on all occasions with all kinds of prayers and requests" (Ephesians 6:18).

Day 3:

IT IS WELL WITH MY SOUL

I think that the dying pray at the last not "please," but "thank you," as a guest thanks his host at the door.
Annie Dillard, *Pilgrim at Tinker Creek*

I have a special affection for an old hymn I first heard in my childhood. I didn't realize how deeply the tune and words to *It Is Well with My Soul* were rooted in my heart until a day in Germany some years ago when I was feeling particularly sorry for myself.

I had enrolled in an "immersion course" at the Goethe Institute to take command of a language that had defeated me in college. The Institute staff went out of their way to make my accommodations pleasant. Instead of assigning me to the dorm where the college-aged students would live, they offered me a room with a family in which the father and mother were my own age. The Asschenfeldt family was gracious enough to offer me all my meals with them and invite me along when they were visiting German friends. None of the other Goethe students had as much opportunity to speak German with natives as I did. But I did not feel grateful. I felt trapped.

One evening I escaped from my host family and walked along a street near a tent revival meeting. A brass ensemble played hymns outside, and I heard the familiar refrain and echo: "It is well (It is well) with my soul (with my soul)." That simple redundant reminder of a truth that had been drowned out by my self-pity made me aware of how truly blessed those weeks in Germany had been.

Sometimes we have to practice being grateful at a time when our feelings don't seem to be up to the task. Perhaps that is what the hymn writer had in mind when he set those words on paper. Horatio Spafford was a successful businessman who faced financial ruin from the great Chicago fire of 1871. Shortly thereafter his four beloved daughters perished when their Europe-bound ship collided with another ship while crossing the Atlantic. Only his wife's life was spared. As Spafford sailed to Europe to join his wife, his own ship passed the place where his daughters had died. As he reached the site, the words to this hymn came to him. Phillip Bliss's tune to which Spafford's words are set—the tune I heard the brass choir play—is called "Ville de Havre" after the ship on which the Spafford children perished.

May Spafford's words and Bliss's lovely tune help you say thank you tonight for all for which you should be grateful.

It Is Well with My Soul

When peace, like a river, attendeth my way,
When sorrows like sea billows roll;
Whatever my lot, Thou has taught me to say,
"It is well, it is well with my soul."

∽∽

Refrain:
It is well with my soul,
It is well with my soul,
It is well, it is well with my soul.

Though Satan should buffet, though trials should come,
Let this blessed assurance control,
That Christ has regarded my helpless estate,
And hath shed His own blood for my soul.

My sin, oh, the bliss of this glorious thought!
My sin—not in part but the whole,
Is nailed to the cross, and I bear it no more,
Praise the Lord, praise the Lord, O my soul!

And Lord, haste the day when my faith shall be sight,
The clouds be rolled back as a scroll;
The trump shall resound, and the Lord shall descend,
"Even so"—it is well with my soul.

Horatio Spafford

 Think about a friend who has endured great suffering in recent times. As you share your own gratitude with God tonight, think, "My heartfelt prayer for you, my very dear friend, is that you may be as healthy and prosperous in every way as you are in soul" (3 John 2 JBP).

Day 4:

HEALING HANDS

I will smile at them and encourage
them to attend to their dreams and so
hear the voices of their inner strangers.
David Hart, The Hippocratic Oath
translated into poetry

I have an occupational hazard as a physician that sometimes crosses over into non-medical areas of my life. It doesn't matter whether I'm in the hospital or on a subway train or worshiping at a church—I always notice physical clues to illness when I look at people. A few years ago while I was in the Chicago area, I found myself diagnosing the congregation when I spoke at a midweek church service.

During the opening moments of the service, I was struck by the sight of a young woman with gnarled fingers. Her shoulders seemed frozen as well, and she was unable to raise her arm above her shoulder. "Ankylosing spondylitis," I thought. "Sad, that she's so terribly afflicted." After the message, the pastor invited anyone who was sick and wanted prayer to come forward and invited me to join him for that prayer time. The young woman, whose name was Gayle, came to me and said, "I'd like you especially to pray with me." And then she told me her story.

My diagnosis was correct. For many years she had suffered from this crippling arthritis. Just that morning her rheumatologist told her that her case was advancing so far that it was time to move up to a type of treatment with more potential for side effects. The drug he had in mind, methotrexate, was most often used as a form of cancer chemotherapy. Gayle was devastated. She came to that service with a mixture of fear and hope. In her sorrow she had prayed that God would send her a sign as to whether or not she should take the medicine. Then she arrived at church and found that the guest speaker was an oncologist, someone intimately familiar with methotrexate and experienced in its use. After the message, she moved as quickly as she could to the front to ask me to pray with her.

I must admit that when I pray with people for their health, I can never completely put my stethoscope away. I found myself doing the same with this suffering young woman. As Gayle suspected, I was very familiar with methotrexate. I could recite its side effects for you with less hesitation than I could rattle off my family members' birthdays! And that's what I found myself doing in prayer. I laid my hand on her cheek to ask God's protection of the lining of her mouth. I touched her back to call down God's mercy on her bone marrow. I laid my hand over her liver, and I touched the skin of her deformed hands. Quietly and thoroughly I went through the side effects her own doctor had outlined for her that morning. But there was a difference this time: we were praying together for God's healing touch.

About six months later I was back in Chicago and saw Gayle in the same church. This time she was up front praying for people. Her right arm was lifted high over her shoulder as she laid her hand on a woman's head. Her arthritis was in remission. Her rheumatologist couldn't believe how well she had responded to methotrexate.

What if Gayle had stayed home that night rather than coming to church for God's healing presence in prayer? Oh, she probably would have taken the methotrexate, but in a spirit of fear. I know many Christians who are afraid to ask God for healing because they believe he has the power to heal but might not choose to free them from their particular illness. For them healing becomes something to be feared rather than embraced. And what if Gayle had chosen to come to church and only ask for prayer for healing from the illness but not for healing from her fear of the recommended treatment? After thirty-five years of caring for children with cancer, I firmly believe that those who see their treatment only in terms of its possible toxic effects experience more side effects than those who see its potential to make them better. *Healing* is only a power word when we give over our fears to God.

Over the years Gayle has had ups and downs with her arthritis, but she has remained steadfast in her commitment to pray for others. One of her special ministries is to pray for doctors. She has had so much personal experience with medical care that she knows our weaknesses and strengths as well as I know methotrexate's risks and benefits. And each time I must tell one of my patients the possible side effects of treatment, I do it in an attitude of prayer.

 Give over any fears you have to God tonight as you pray, "Heal me, O LORD, and I will be healed; save me and I will be saved, for you are the one I praise" (Jeremiah 17:14).

Day 5:

THE CHURCH IN LIVING COLOR

If you wish to see the holy Christian church depicted in living colors, and given a living form, in a painting in miniature, then place the Book of Psalms in front of you.
Martin Luther, *Preface to the Psalms*

I am curious about Luther's comparison of the Psalms to the church. His prose is almost as magnificent as the holy literature he commends to our reading.

In one sense, Luther challenges us to dig out the ways in which we see the church imaged in each psalm. Although it is tempting to dissect metaphors and analyze them, I prefer instead to take the inspired metaphor of marriage that Paul used to describe Christ's love for his church. Keep the Holy Spirit's words through Paul to the little church in Ephesus in mind as you read Psalm 16 tonight: "Christ loved the church and gave himself up for her to make her holy, cleansing her by the washing with water through the word, and to present her to himself as a radiant church, without stain or wrinkle or any other blemish, but holy and blameless. . . . This is a profound mystery—but I am talking about Christ and the church" (Ephesians 5:26–27, 32).

PSALM 16

Keep me safe, O God,
>   for in you I take refuge.

❧

I said to the LORD, "You are my Lord;
>   apart from you I have no good thing."
As for the saints who are in the land,
>   they are the glorious ones in whom is all my delight.
The sorrows of those will increase
>   who run after other gods.
I will not pour out their libations of blood
>   or take up their names on my lips.

❧

LORD, you have assigned me my portion and my cup;
>   you have made my lot secure.
The boundary lines have fallen for me in pleasant places;
>   surely I have a delightful inheritance.

❧

I will praise the LORD, who counsels me;
>   even at night my heart instructs me.
I have set the LORD always before me.
>   Because he is at my right hand,
>   I will not be shaken.

Therefore my heart is glad and my tongue rejoices;
    my body also will rest secure,
because you will not abandon me to the grave,
    nor will you let your Holy One see decay.
You have made known to me the path of life;
    you will fill me with joy in your presence,
    with eternal pleasures at your right hand.

 Choose a color to paint your home church in your dreams tonight, knowing the sweet closeness of Christ as you repeat, "My body also will rest secure" (Psalm 16:9).

Day 6:

NIGHT

God speaks ... in a dream, in a vision of the night, when deep sleep falls on mortals, while they slumber in their beds.
Job 33:14–15 NRSV

I have been so busy with other things in the last few years that I have neglected my lovely home. This weekend, I whacked at the weeds and reclaimed a garden area I can see from my bedroom balcony. To top it off, I placed a squirrel-proof bird feeder and a small birdbath on the deck. I want to go to sleep at night knowing that I'll wake up to little chirping friends who beat me to the sunrise.

But I have you, my readers, to thank for that. When I selected this lovely poem by William Blake for your enjoyment this evening, I got to thinking about some chores I needed to do. May Blake's words bring deep, perfect peace to the close of your evening and waken you to friendly noises of nature.

NIGHT

The sun descending in the west,
The evening star does shine.
The birds are silent in their nest,

And I must seek for mine,
The moon like a flower,
In heavens high bower;
With silent delight,
Sits and smiles on the night.

Farewell green fields and happy grove,
Where flocks have took delight.
Where lambs have nibbled, silent moves
The feet of angels bright;
Unseen they pour blessing,
And joy without ceasing,
On each bud and blossom,
And each sleeping bosom.

They took in every thoughtless nest,
Where birds are coverd warm;
They visit caves of every beast,
To keep them all from harm;
If they see any weeping,
That should have been sleeping
They pour sleep on their head
And sit down by their bed.

When wolves and tygers howl for prey
They pitying stand and weep;
Seeking to drive their thirst away,

And keep them from the sheep.
But if they rush dreadful;
The angels most heedful,
Receive each mild spirit,
New worlds to inherit.

⚬

And there the lions ruddy eyes,
Shall flow with tears of gold:
And pitying the tender cries,
And walking round the fold:
Saying: wrath by his meekness
And by his health, sickness,
Is driven away,
From our immortal day.

⚬

And now beside thee bleating lamb,
I can lie down and sleep;
Or think on him who bore thy name,
Graze after thee and weep.
For wash'd in lifes river,
My bright mane for ever,
Shall shine like the gold,
As I guard o'er the fold.

William Blake[3]

Use spiritual eyes to acknowledge the presence of God's angels surrounding you as you sleep, repeating, "He will put you in his angels' charge to guard you wherever you go" (Psalm 91:11 JB).

Day 7:

THE FIRST SONG
OF ISAIAH

*Before Isaiah had left the middle court,
the word of the LORD came to him.*

2 Kings 20:4

Moses complained that his speech was slow, but Isaiah mourned that his own speech was unclean. In a heavenly vision that sealed Isaiah's calling to be a prophet, a seraph touched his lips with a live coal. Cleansed and set apart for God's work, Isaiah was ready to sing about the new work God had planned for his people.

THE FIRST SONG OF ISAIAH (ECCE, DEUS)

In that day you will say: . . .

"Surely God is my salvation;
 I will trust and not be afraid.
The LORD, the LORD, is my strength and my song;
 he has become my salvation."
With joy you will draw water
 from the wells of salvation.

In that day you will say:

"Give thanks to the LORD, call on his name;
     make known among the nations what he has done,
     and proclaim that his name is exalted.
Sing to the LORD, for he has done glorious things;
     let this be known to all the world.
Shout aloud and sing for joy, people of Zion,
     for great is the Holy One of Israel among you."

Isaiah 12

*Glory be to the Father, and to the Son, and to the Holy Spirit:
As it was in the beginning, is now, and will be for ever. Amen.*

*Think about some of the names for the Lord that
express his greatness as you repeat, "Declare his
doings among the people, make mention that his
name is exalted" (Isaiah 12:4 KJV).*

3

IMPORTANT REST

In music, the rests are just as important as the notes.

Donald Toney

Day 1:

THE BURDEN-LIFTING DREAM

*There are no rules of architecture for
a castle in the clouds.*

G. K. Chesterton

Like many others running on empty at bedtime, I tend to take my burdens to bed with me. One particular dream has come to me on those nights when I've exhausted myself about a problem I can't seem to solve. This dream not only spells out a solution to my problem but also brings a feeling of relief.

To get to my destination, I have to go through deep, dark woods at night with no flashlight to help me find my way. A friend comes along, a child psychiatrist who has helped many children. He offers to carry me the rest of the way through the woods. After I get to my destination, I tell another friend about the fearsome journey. While I'm telling him the story, I feel the relief of my burden being lifted from my shoulders. In my dream I think, "Why don't I tell a friend tomorrow what's bothering me? I might feel a lot better if I didn't carry this burden by myself."

Lying awake fretting doesn't give God the chance to take a burden away from me. Only under the sweet, healing influence of sleep do I have the chance to solve these problems.

So often we quote the words "[his] yoke is easy and [his] burden is light" (Matthew 11:30) or sing those words in Handel's *Messiah* without remembering the context in which Jesus said them.

Here's a trick I use sometimes when I can't fall asleep because of unfinished business that's bothering me. I list those things in my prayer journal and make an arrow ➔ to turn them over to God. The conscious act of making the list helps me refuse further thoughts about those problems before I fall asleep.

 As you fall asleep this evening, hear Jesus' invitation, "Come to me. Get away with me and you'll recover your life. I'll show you how to take a real rest" (Matthew 11:28 MSG).

Day 2:

A MARTYR'S PRAYER

It was a test we would all hope to pass,
but none of us want to take.
Michael W. Smith

When I was a child, I read Foxe's *Book of Martyrs* with the same relish that I might read a Michael Crichton novel today. It doesn't get much more spine-chilling than Foxe's roast 'em, toast 'em, serve 'em up to the lions stories. But I never thought that the early Christian martyrs' stories had anything to do with me personally.

I live in America, thank you, with a church on every corner and a constitution to protect my religious rights. The worst martyrship I could imagine would be to die in the course of my medical work in some distant land from some Ebola-like illness. But even that form of death would have paled by comparison to the persecution Foxe described. I would not, for example, have thought to invite an African mosquito to bite me because I'm a Christian.

Ignatius of Antioch, born shortly after the life of Christ, was bishop of the Christian community in Syria. After his arrest and deportation to Rome for sentencing, he wrote letters to churches in Asia Minor in which he anticipated his coming martyrdom. "May I be ground by the teeth of the wild beasts until I become the fine white bread that belongs to Christ," he wrote.

As much as I would like to think that things like that cannot happen to Christians in America, it has happened here. Cassie Bernall had not been a Christian for long when she faced just such a situation. Huddled with classmates on the library floor of Columbine High School during a mass shooting, Cassie heard one of the gunmen ask her, "Do you believe in God?" After she told him that she did believe in God, he shot her to death.*

To bring martyrdom into my century makes it too plausible, evoking the possibility that someone like me might be pulverized for Christ. My problem is that I love this world so much that I can think of countless Christian reasons why I should continue to live. But here's what Jesus said: "I tell you the truth, unless a kernel of wheat falls to the ground and dies, it remains only a single seed. But if it dies, it produces many seeds" (John 12:24).

Ignatius became the fine white bread for Jesus that he longed to be. Cassie's story has produced more seeds for Christ than she could have if she had survived. In my living or in my dying, just how "crusty" am I?

 The ultimate goal of all prayer is to come into the presence of God. Consider how seriously you want to achieve that goal as you repeat, "To me, to live is Christ and to die is gain" (Philippians 1:21).

---

*Cassie's mother tells her story in *She Said Yes: The Unlikely Martyrdom of Cassie Bernall* (Farmington: Plough, 1999).

Day 3:

HE WHO BEGAN A GOOD WORK IN YOU

Oh God, I really don't know how it works, but it works!

Kin Lam

Blessed are they who have songs in the night, for insomnia shall ne'er destroy them. Those of us subject to sleepless nights can use vesper hymns to slide into sleep.

For the last few years I've left a Christian station on the radio overnight playing softly while I try to fall asleep. Sometimes I find beautiful worship songs incorporated into my dreams. Other times, when I wake up in the middle of the night, I hear a message in song that helps me get back to sleep.

That's exactly what was happening a few years back when I was getting ready to go to Marburg, Germany, for a year's sabbatical away from my duties at Yale. There were so many things to do that I didn't seem able to put my list away when I went to sleep. Then one night I woke to hear Jon Mohr's familiar chorus:

He who began a good work in you,
He who began a good work in you,

He is faithful to complete it.
He is faithful to complete it.
He who started the work
Will be faithful to complete it in you. [4]

That was just the word I needed right then. Thanks to the song, I went promptly back to sleep. But the story doesn't end there.

On Sunday nights in Marburg we held an English worship service in a house above a jazz club. An unfamiliar young man came to the service one night with a saxophone in hand. Karl had come to town to visit the jazz club but hadn't found a jam session happening down there. Then he saw the sign for our English worship service and wandered in.

Karl had recently become a Christian himself and was working for a Christian radio station. We invited him to join our small worship band that night. He was a good saxophonist, and I mean *really good!*

After the service he told me how he had come to faith and how worried he was because he wasn't as good a Christian as most of the people he knew at the radio station where he worked. You know, baby Christian type of talk.

I couldn't get this young man out of my mind. The next day I saw a coworker of his and scrawled the text to Philippians 1:6 in German on a piece of paper. I asked her to give Karl the note when she next saw him at work.

When I saw Karl a few days later, he was very excited. His pastor had given him Philippians 1:6 on a previous occasion when Karl had indicated frustration with his spiritual progress. He accepted my note as an indication that God really wanted him to believe this promise that God would keep working in his life.

Even in our so-called moments of defeat, God is there with us, working. God was present for me and with me in my insomnia. He was there with Karl in his spiritual growing pains. He is there for you as well, working out what he faithfully promised to bring to completion.

Think about an area of your life which you have considered a defeat. Paint a picture in your mind of God turning it into a victory as you repeat, "Being confident of this, that he who began a good work in me will carry it on to completion until the day of Christ Jesus" (Philippians 1:6, adapted).

Day 4:

TURNING ZEROS INTO HEROES

Most books on success tell you that you have really "arrived" when you win the race. That's wrong. Truly successful people are the ones who help others cross the finish line.

Dave Thomas, *Well Done*

It beats all human logic why I became a specialist for children with cancer. Back when I began my career, most of the children I cared for died from that dreaded disease. But during my tour of duty in the war on cancer, things have changed dramatically. Praise God, 58 percent fewer children die from cancer today than when I first started in the field.

Sometimes I ask myself, "What if I had counted all those kids as zeros, and didn't have the power to believe that each and every one could be a survivor?" For one thing, we would have 350 less "long-term survivors" of childhood cancer in our practice at Yale, including a young woman named Jackie.

There was a time in Jackie's life when it wasn't at all clear that she would live to finish high school. This week she brought her adopted son James in to meet me, and I got to hold him in my arms. I suspect that back in Korea someone thought James wasn't worth counting, but with his new parents James has a wonderful future. It takes a zero-turned-hero to spot the potential in others and be kind enough to believe in their future.

Meet my friend Mary Taylor Previte, who was imprisoned by the Japanese during World War II. At the New Jersey juvenile detention facility Mary directs, the kids wonder what a respectable white lady like her is doing in a jail like theirs. She calls these lost children her "hungry ghosts." Mary feeds them with respect and teaches them about self-control. She shows her kids that even if the world has given up on them, they can find their way out of the hellhole she has chosen to share with them. She treats these "zeros" with respect and discharges guards who don't do the same. "Can I tell you a story?" Mary asks two of her young charges. They nod, and they listen to her story. Two more out-of-control lives are given the opportunity to change. [5]

Dale Cryderman is another person you'd like to know. This public high school teacher speaks unblushingly about his love for "his kids." For thirty-five years Dale has taught them high school chemistry, but he has also taught them about Jesus through the way he lives his life. More than any other year, Dale is looking forward to getting back to school this fall. He's been through cancer surgery this summer. When sleep evades him, Dale searches Scripture for words like *rest* and *peace* and *safety.* These are words kids search for too. Dale falls back to sleep praying lovingly over the list of students he'll meet next month when school starts again. He visualizes his students in the lecture room and lab and starts praying for each of them by name.

What about you? Do you know any young zeros waiting for someone in step with the power of God to help them feel safe, to help them survive? You don't have to be a doctor, a prison administrator, or a teacher to make a marked difference in a kid's life. You need just enough strength to embrace one fragile child.

 Picture a child whose life you can touch as you recite, "The fruit of the Spirit is love, joy, peace, patience, kindness, goodness, faithfulness, gentleness and self-control" (Galatians 5:22–23).

Day 5:
A Glimpse of
Daddy's Face

*Spare me the theology; just give me
the story.*

Tom Winton, "Image: A Journal of
Religion and the Arts"

I love a touching story Maxie Dunham tells about a small lad who lost his mom. Barely able to contain his own grief on the day of his wife's funeral, the young father had to deal with questions from his little son.

"Daddy," he heard in the darkness that night, "Daddy, where is Mommy?"

Is there any satisfactory answer to such a question? But a child's questions deserve truthful answers. Best as he could, the daddy tried to explain to his son what had happened. But the question kept coming back to him from the boy, "Where is Mommy? When is she coming home?"

Finally, the father brought the child to his own bed. If his words could not comfort, perhaps his presence could. Then, in the darkness, he felt a small hand touching his face.

"Daddy, is your face toward me?" The last words the child spoke before falling asleep were, "If your face is toward me, I think I can go to sleep."[6]

David asks God the same question in Psalm 27. His life is in danger. He is living in the middle of a war zone. But David knows the secret for sleep.

PSALM 27

The LORD is my light and my salvation—
    whom shall I fear?
The LORD is the stronghold of my life—
    of whom shall I be afraid?
When evil men advance against me
    to devour my flesh,
when my enemies and my foes attack me,
    they will stumble and fall.
Though an army besiege me,
    my heart will not fear;
though war break out against me,
    even then will I be confident.

One thing I ask of the LORD,
    this is what I seek:
that I may dwell in the house of the LORD
    all the days of my life,
to gaze upon the beauty of the LORD
    and to seek him in his temple.
For in the day of trouble
    he will keep me safe in his dwelling;

he will hide me in the shelter of his tabernacle
>   and set me high upon a rock.
Then my head will be exalted
>   above the enemies who surround me;
at his tabernacle will I sacrifice with shouts of joy;
>   I will sing and make music to the LORD.

⌒◞

Hear my voice when I call, O LORD;
>   be merciful to me and answer me.
My heart says of you, "Seek his face!"
>   Your face, LORD, I will seek.
Do not hide your face from me,
>   do not turn your servant away in anger;
>   you have been my helper.
Do not reject me or forsake me,
>   O God my Savior.
Though my father and mother forsake me,
>   the LORD will receive me.
Teach me your way, O LORD;
>   lead me in a straight path
>   because of my oppressors.
Do not turn me over to the desire of my foes,
>   for false witnesses rise up against me,
>   breathing out violence.

⌒◞

I am still confident of this:
>   I will see the goodness of the LORD
>   in the land of the living.

Wait for the LORD;
    be strong and take heart
    and wait for the LORD.

 As you fall asleep tonight, say to your Abba, "Do not hide your face from me" (Psalm 27:9).

Day 6:

LUCIFER

*There is a Moment in each Day that
Satan cannot find.*

William Blake

Some of my friends who have difficulty with bedtime devotions use the phrase "under siege" to describe their nightmare nighttimes. Although they sense God's presence with them by day, somehow they feel that the night belongs to the enemy of their soul. Parents often feel that way when their children stray.

Have you ever wondered whether evil is an impersonal force, and questioned whether there is a personal devil? If I ever had any doubts, they vanished the day one of my patients died. Randy was two years old when he was diagnosed with leukemia, seven when he nearly died during a bone marrow transplant. Once when he nearly died, he saw angels standing at his bedside. But where were the angels last weekend when Randy went to a friend's house? He never recovered from a drug-induced coma to report what he saw and heard. Dead from drugs at nineteen after surviving leukemia!

How personal that evil feels to me. Someone would have to hate his parents with a cosmic venom to bring them to this point by such a tortuous path!

The following stanza taken from Act V of a poetic drama by Joost van den Vondel depicts the triumphant battle in heaven waged by the forces of Light on behalf of us who are created in the image of God. If you are facing any spiritual battles tonight, let van den Vondel's encouraging words help you win. As personal as evil may seem tonight, remember that the God who will be the final victor wants to know you personally too.

LUCIFER

MICHAEL: Praise be to God! The state of things above
Has changed. Our Grand Foe has met his defeat;
And in our hands he leaves his standard, helm,
And morning-star, and shield and banners bold.
Which spoil, gained in pursuit, even now does hang,
'Mid joys triumphant, honors, songs of praise,
And sounds of trump, on Heaven's axis bright,
The mirror clear of all rebelliousness,
Of all ambition that would rear its crest
'Gainst God, the stem immovable—grand fount,
Prime source, and Father of all things that are,
Which from His hand their nature did receive,
And various attributes. No more shall we
Behold the glow of Majesty Supreme
Dimmed by the damp of base ingratitude.
There, deep beneath our sigh and these high thrones,
They wander through the air and restlessly
Move to and fro, all blind and overcast
With shrouding clouds, and horribly deformed.
Thus is his fate, who would assail God's Throne.

CHORUS: Thus is his fate, who would assail God's Throne.
Thus his fate, who would, through envy, man
In God's own image made, deprive of light.

Joost van den Vondel[7]

 As you fall asleep tonight, remember that when Christ returns, "there will be no more night . . . for the Lord God will give them light" (Revelation 22:5).

Day 7:

THE SECOND SONG OF ISAIAH

Isaiah did not send you to a bath, there to wash away murder and other sins which not even all the water of the sea were sufficient to purge: but as might have been expected, this was that saving bath of olden time which followed those who repented by faith through the blood of Christ.

Justin Martyr

At the age of thirty, pagan philosopher Justin Martyr was converted to Christianity by reading Scripture. Impressed by the steadfast spirit of Christian martyrs, Justin listened to an elderly saint explain how Jesus was the promised fulfillment of the Jewish prophets. "Straightway a flame was kindled in my soul," said Justin, "and a love of the prophets and those who are friends of Christ possessed me."

THE SECOND SONG OF ISAIAH (QUAERITE DOMINUM)

Seek the LORD while he may be found;
    call on him while he is near.
Let the wicked forsake his way
    and the evil man his thoughts;
Let them turn to the LORD, and he will have mercy on him,
    and to our God, for he will freely pardon.

❧

"For my thoughts are not your thoughts,
    neither are your ways my ways,"
        declares the LORD.
"As the heavens are higher than the earth,
    so are my ways higher than your ways,
    and my thoughts than your thoughts.
As the rain and the snow
    come down from heaven,
and do not return to it
    without watering the earth
and making it bud and flourish,
    so that it yields seed for the sower and bread for the eater,
so is my word that goes out from my mouth:
    It will not return to me empty,
but will accomplish what I desire
    and achieve the purpose for which I sent it."

Isaiah 55:6–11

Glory be to the Father, and to the Son,
    and to the Holy Spirit:
As it was in the beginning,
    is now, and will be for ever. Amen.

Think about what God's word has accomplished in your life today as you repeat, "So shall my word be that goeth forth out of my mouth: It shall not return unto me void, but it shall accomplish that which I please, and it shall prosper in the thing whereto I sent it" (Isaiah 55:11 KJV).

4

DELIGHTFUL SACRIFICE

A verse may find him who a sermon flies,
And turn delight into sacrifice.
George Herbert, *The Church Door*

Day 1:

THE BRIDGING DREAM

The ladder is long, it is strong and well made; has stood hundreds of years and is not yet decayed; many millions have climbed it and reached Zion's hill, many millions by faith now are climbing it still.

From an eighteenth-century English carol

Aldo and Scotty were not the only children I met in the hospital who successfully integrated the spiritual realm with the world they knew here on earth. As children reached out to God, they incorporated tokens of their concrete, everyday earthly days into their dreams. They were building sturdy bridges from earth to heaven.

Bridging dreams often come to us just at the time we most need to be touched by the holy. In "A Window to Heaven" I described a boy who saw Jesus in a dream shortly before he died. Although his parents weren't believers, Jesus came to him on a big yellow school bus to carry him to heaven.[8] He accepted Jesus' invitation. I was going through a dreadful time myself when I had this wonderful dream:

I was riding in a small plane when it started to have engine trouble. The pilot warned us to prepare for a crash landing. Mirac-

ulously, we landed with only minor damage to the plane. After we landed, I looked around and realized that we had landed in a place that was familiar to me but not to my fellow passengers.

Marburg, Germany! Here I was in my "home away from home."* The pilot told us that the repairs would be made quickly, and that we would not be on the ground very long. There may not be time for sightseeing, but I wanted to share what I knew about Marburg with my fellow passengers. What limited features about this medieval town should I mention?

I was filled with warmth as memories of my times in Marburg flooded over me. I pointed out the window to the castle on top of the mountain, bathed in warm gold sunlight. "Isn't that the most beautiful sight you have ever seen?" I asked the other passengers.

The telephone woke me up from this dream. I thought, "Oh, no! This is no time to wake up. I want to stay in this dream."

Marburg is my golden Jerusalem, my holy city, the place where I don't want to hang up my harp on the first willow tree I spot (Psalm 137:2). I'd rather be singing in Marburg than talking to a case manager for an HMO who wants to refuse my Aldos and Scotties the care they need and deserve. But here I am, back in my "Babylon" where I just want to sit down and weep. Why did the phone have to wake me up now?

Despite all the reminders of my daily life, I had to admit that it was a beautiful dream that deserved to be remembered. Its images nourished my soul that day, and built a bridge back to the place I call my spiritual home. The dream reminded me to take those things I learned in my "Jerusalem" and to use them to comfort those whom I care for on earth.

---

*See *Breakfast for the Heart.*

May God span the gap between earth and heaven for you tonight as you repeat, "As a mother comforts her child, so I will comfort you; you shall be comforted in Jerusalem" (Isaiah 66:13 NRSV).

Day 2:

THE LORD'S PRAYER

The prayer preceding all prayers is
"May it be the real I who speaks. May
it be the real Thou that I speak to."
C. S. Lewis, *Letters to Malcolm*

The prayer that follows, which includes the Lord's Prayer, was recorded at an anniversary service for ushers at the New Jerusalem African Methodist Episcopal Church in Wadmalaw, South Carolina. It was transcribed with the congregational responses—"more groans than words"—included in italics. There is no doubt that it was the real James Brown who was praying to the real God!

OPENING PRAYER FOR THE USHER'S ANNIVERSARY

Our Father who art in heaven
Hallowed be thy name
Thy kingdom come, Lord
Let thy holy and righteous
Will be done on this earth
As your will was already done in heaven
Give us, Lord, this day
As our daily bread
You forgive those who have sin

And trespass against us *Amen.*
Lead us not into sin, neither temptation
But, please deliver us from evil *Yes!*
O Lord, that thine may be our kingdom
We expecting your kingdom to be
[A] poor sinner['] glory *O yeah! . . .*
Don't leave us alone to oneself *Uh uh,*
Neither in the hands of the wicked man *Ah yeah!*
Lead us though in the tempting of old Satan *Oh yeah!*
Have mercy if thou, on us so please.
We are here this evening, Jesus *Oh yeah.*
We can't do nothing without you *Uh huh*
Come Holy Spirit, Heavenly Dove *Oh yeah*
With all thou quickening power *Power!*
Kindle the flame of our Savior's love *Yeah!*
In these cold hearts of ours *Cold . . .*
Want you to meet me Jesus . . .
And my soul have rest *Rest*
Tis thy servant's prayer, Master!
Amen. *Amen! Amen! Yeah! Yeah! Sir! All right!*
                          James Brown, adapted[9]

*Be specific about a fault of your own as you repeat,
"Forgive us our sins, for we also forgive everyone
who sins against us" (Luke 11:4).*

Day 3:

YOU ARE BEAUTIFUL BEYOND DESCRIPTION

Perhaps I am so fascinated by his face because the Scriptures make no mention of it. Precisely because it is not mentioned, all its details are left to my imagination ... if ever I had a sleepless night, his beautiful face would rise up in my heart.

Shusako Endo, *Silence*

A wise man once noted that there are three stages to life: youth, middle age, and "you're looking wonderful." As much as we smile at that third stage (especially when it's our own age-stage!), we would have an even better reason to smile if with each passing year we grew into the likeness of Jesus.

Mark Altrogge's lovely song invites us into the presence of our "looking wonderful" Lord.

I STAND IN AWE

You are beautiful beyond description,
Too marvelous for words,
Too wonderful for comprehension—
Like nothing ever seen or heard.

      ❧

Who can grasp your infinite wisdom?
Who can fathom the depths of your love?
You are beautiful beyond description,
Majesty enthroned above.

      ❧

And I stand, I stand in awe of you,
I stand, I stand in awe of you,
Holy God to whom all praise is due,
I stand in awe of you.

Mark Altrogge[10]

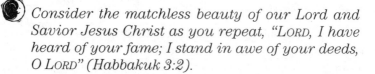 *Consider the matchless beauty of our Lord and Savior Jesus Christ as you repeat, "LORD, I have heard of your fame; I stand in awe of your deeds, O LORD" (Habbakuk 3:2).*

Day 4:

STEEL-GRID POSSIBILITIES

We tend to make courage too dramatic.
Courage is often doing something sim-
ple, unpleasant, or boring again and
again until we get it down pat.
Dave Thomas, *Well Done*

If you read *Breakfast for the Heart*, you know that I am not very fond of bridges. I am a pure case of white knuckles when up against a narrow, high-arching span or a steel-grid deck. I've been known to add one hundred miles to a journey to avoid one of my most terrifying bridges. I've even pulled over and asked a passenger to drive over a bridge, and resumed driving when we were safe on the other side. I can't give you any explanation for this phobia, and I haven't noticed that applying logic to the situation has brought any relief. It defies logic, therefore, why I got on Interstate 95 one Sunday morning and drove to a church that is an hour from my home and lies beyond one of my most feared bridges.

The time had come for me to part company with my church of fifteen years and move on. But it wasn't an easy matter to choose another church. For a month of Sundays I had visited various churches near my home but had not found the combination of worship and teaching that I was hoping to call home. Then, one Sunday morning, I remembered a pastor with whom I had worked a decade before. The church, however, was an hour from my home and the denomination was not one I had ever embraced. And then there was the matter of the steel-deck bridge on the Merritt Parkway. Without a passenger to help me cross the bridge, I took a deep breath and white-knuckled it over, doing little Lamaze-like pants. How glad I am that I braved it! Grace Church became my home.

Well, I admit that for the first month I found a detour that added ten miles to each direction, but it substituted a low, flat, wide bridge without a steel deck. Finally I began to focus on what lay beyond the bridge, not the means to get there. What if I had allowed *bridge* to remain a fear word, and not a word impregnated with power? For one thing, I would have missed five years of sound teaching, supportive saints, and meaningful worship. Healed of my white knuckles, I now courageously sail across the bridge on my way to Grace.

 Whatever "bridge" in your life you're having trouble crossing, see yourself passing safely over tonight as you recite, "The LORD is my strength and my song; he has become my salvation" (Exodus 15:2).

Day 5:

THE ANSWER HAD BETTER BE GOOD

The Psalms allow me better to pray
over the news, making me go deeper
with what I read in the daily paper.
Kathleen Norris, *The Psalms*

A teen friend is mighty perturbed about what she's reading in the newspapers lately. There are too many stories of teenagers gunning down teachers and classmates in school. After one episode too many, her pastor planned a special youth group meeting to talk about these things. My young friend is going armed with questions. "The answers had better be good," she warns me.

I have the same feeling when I watch the ten o'clock news each night before going to bed. On an average day you hear about senseless violence from coast to coast, juveniles tried as adults for heinous crimes, and politicians caught in immoral behavior. When I pick up the Bible, I agree that the answers had better be good!

Poet Kathleen Norris invites us to go deeper into the Psalms to understand the heart of God in our crazy circumstances. In Psalm 55 she reads of violence and strife in the city. "Like the psalmist, I can raise a hope that those who profit by doing evil will come to understand that God has in fact 'set [them] in slippery places' (Psalm 73:18). And when human savagery reaches catastrophic proportions, turning even religious sanctuaries into places of massacre, the psalmist's outcry in Psalm 79—'Their blood have they shed like water round about Jerusalem; and there was none to bury them' (Psalm 79:3)— gives witness that sometimes the power to name, to describe, and to lament is the only power we have."[11]

What story in the world is troubling you tonight? Give it a name and turn that name over to God as you read this psalm.

PSALM 55

Listen to my prayer, O God,
> do not ignore my plea;
> hear me and answer me.
My thoughts trouble me and I am distraught
> at the voice of the enemy,
> at the stares of the wicked;
for they bring down suffering upon me
> and revile me in their anger.

⁓

My heart is in anguish within me;
> the terrors of death assail me.
Fear and trembling have beset me;
> horror has overwhelmed me.
I said, "Oh, that I had the wings of a dove!
> I would fly away and be at rest—
I would flee far away
> and stay in the desert;
I would hurry to my place of shelter,
> far from the tempest and storm."

Confuse the wicked, O Lord, confound their speech,
    for I see violence and strife in the city.
Day and night they prowl about on its walls;
    malice and abuse are within it.
Destructive forces are at work in the city;
    threats and lies never leave its streets.

If an enemy were insulting me,
    I could endure it;
if a foe were raising himself against me,
    I could hide from him.
But it is you, a man like myself,
    my companion, my close friend,
with whom I once enjoyed sweet fellowship
    as we walked with the throng at the house of God.

Let death take my enemies by surprise;
    let them go down alive to the grave,
    for evil finds lodging among them.

But I call to God,
    and the LORD saves me.
Evening, morning and noon
    I cry out in distress,
    and he hears my voice.

He ransoms me unharmed
>from the battle waged against me,
even though many oppose me.
God, who is enthroned forever,
will hear them and afflict them—
men who never change their ways
and have no fear of God.

～

My companion attacks his friends;
he violates his covenant.
His speech is smooth as butter,
yet war is in his heart;
his words are more soothing than oil,
yet they are drawn swords.

～

Cast your cares on the LORD
and he will sustain you;
he will never let the righteous fall.
But you, O God, will bring down the wicked
into the pit of corruption;
bloodthirsty and deceitful men
will not live out half their days.

～

But as for me, I trust in you.

As you fall asleep tonight, mentally close the newspaper and turn off the TV as you repeat, "Cast your cares on the LORD and he will sustain you" (Psalm 55:22).

Day 6:

CIRCLES

He sits enthroned above the circle of
the earth.

Isaiah 40:22

Luci Shaw, one of only two living poets I quote in this collection, has the gift of finding profound beauty in simple objects. Hear what Luci has to say about circles.

CIRCLES

I sing of circles, rounded things,
    apples and wreaths and wedding rings,
    and domes and spheres,
    and falling tears,
    well-rounded meals,
    water wheels,
    bottom of bells
    or walled-in wells;
    rain dropping, golden in the air
    or silver on your shining hair;
    pebbles in pewter-colored ponds

making circles, rounds on rounds;
the curve of a repeating rhyme;
the circle of the face of time.
Beyond these circles I can see
the circle of eternity.

*

Does passing of each season fair
make of the four a noble square?
No. For to each the others lend
a cyclic, curving, rhythmic blend.
Remember, spring in summer gone
comes round again. New spring comes on.

*

The circle in the eagle's eye
mirrors the circle of the sky,
the blue horizon, end to end,
end to end,
over earth's never-ending bend.

*

The arc of love from God to men
orbiting, goes to him again.
My love, to loving God above,
captures *me* in the round of love.

Luci Shaw[12]

What is your favorite rounded thing? Hold that image in your heart as you fall asleep contemplating the eternal nature of God's love for you, repeating, "He has made everything beautiful in its time. He has also set eternity in the human heart" (Ecclesiastes 3:11 RNIV).

Day 7:

THE THIRD SONG OF ISAIAH

*Isaiah said this because he saw Jesus'
glory and spoke about him.*

John 12:41

In a song celebrating the glorious restoration of Jerusalem, the holy city of the holy God, Isaiah speaks of Israel's evangelistic mission as a light to all nations.

THE THIRD SONG OF ISAIAH (SURGE, ILLUMINARE)

Arise, shine, for your light has come,
    and the glory of the LORD rises upon you.
See, darkness covers the earth
    and thick darkness is over the peoples,
but the LORD rises upon you
    and his glory appears over you.
Nations will come to your light,
    and kings to the brightness of your dawn....

Your gates will always stand open;
    they will never be shut, day or night. . . .

∝∝

All who despise you will bow down at your feet
and will call you the City of the LORD,
    Zion of the Holy One of Israel. . . .

∝∝

No longer will violence be heard in your land,
    nor ruin or destruction within your borders,
but you will call your walls Salvation
    and your gates Praise.
The sun will no more be your light by day,
    nor will the brightness of the moon shine on you,
for the LORD will be your everlasting light,
    and your God will be your glory.
Isaiah 60:1–3, 11, 14, 18–19

*Glory be to the Father, and to the Son,
    and to the Holy Spirit:
As it was in the beginning, is now,
    and will be for ever. Amen.*

 *How did God shed light on your day today? Think
about that as you repeat, "The LORD will be your
everlasting light, and your God will be your glory"
(Isaiah 60:19).*

5

PASTORAL PAGEANTRY

All of this pageantry is conveyed to my heart and mind when I repeat the simple statement, "He restoreth my soul."
Philip Keller, *A Shepherd Looks at Psalm 23*

Day 1:

THE INSTRUCTIONAL DREAM

I've dreamed in my life dreams that have stayed with me ever after and changed my ideas; they've gone through me like wine through water, and altered the color of my mind.
Emily Brontë, *Wuthering Heights*

It was the night before a big exam in medical school when I had the most awful dream I could imagine. Fifty percent of my class had failed the first half of this course, and I was scheduled for an oral exam with a fearful professor. In my dream, he asked me questions about the rare disease that was his specialty. How unfair, I thought. He knows more about sarcoidosis than anyone in the world and he expects me to know everything he knows about it? How many cases am I likely to see in a lifetime of medical practice? Mercilessly, he pounded me with one question after another in my dream. My mind scrambled searching for the answers. I woke up with the telltale signs of a nightmare. Heart racing. Sweat pouring. Not a very nice way to start what promised to be a difficult day.

None of my classmates looked very happy that morning. We huddled in the cafeteria drinking coffee and poring over class notes rather than talking to each other. When the time came, I walked slowly toward the dreaded office door and timidly knocked. A booming voice yelled, "Come in!"

He motioned me to a chair, smiling. I took my place. He spun in his swivel chair to face me. He folded his hands and twiddled his thumbs. "What would you like to talk about today?" he asked.

What would I like to talk about? He had turned the tables on me. Let me name my own poison. He wasn't going to ask me about sarcoidosis after all! That was no prophetic dream, just a nightmare last night. As quickly as these thoughts raced through my mind, I had another thought.

"Why don't we talk about sarcoidosis?" I politely suggested.

He broke out in a grin and said, "Yes, why don't we?"

Following the line of inquisition in my dream, I fleshed out the most important points in the pathology of sarcoidosis. When I finished, he leaned back and said, "Well done. And you get extra points for chutzpah."

That dream was an instructional experience on many levels. Telling you this story now, I can't recall how I found the nerve to ask for my greatest fear. But as I lectured the world's expert on his specialty, I realized that in my dream I had reviewed what he had taught me about that disease. The middle-of-the-night review had even provided me with a logical outline around which to structure my words. During my waking hours, knowing who would be examining me, I hadn't the courage to study up on the subject. In the safe comfort of my dream, I finally accomplished what needed to be done.

Nightmares can only be nightmarish if we allow them to be. If we run away from them, the way I wanted to run away from this professor, we'll never learn about our own capacity for courage.

Can you remember a dream that came true because you carried your courage over to your waking hours? Think about the lesson of that dream as you "let the prophet who has a dream tell his dream, but let the one who has my word speak it faithfully" (Jeremiah 23:28).

Day 2:

GOURMET PRAYER

They feast on the abundance of your house; you give them drink from your river of delights.

Psalm 36:8

My friend Linda is a talented and dedicated hostess who loves to plan a lavish dinner party. Frankly, Linda's gourmet meals are rather intimidating. If you ask her for a recipe, she will recite a forty-hour work week of preparation for each course. Perhaps it was my reaction to Linda's strategy that inspired me to write my as-yet unpublished cookbook, *Gourmet Cooking for the Overcommitted*.

In my kitchen I achieve the same goals as work-weary Linda with only a fraction of her effort. My guests also feast in delight. But rather than intimidate those who want to imitate my cookery, I remove as many obstacles as possible to their personal success. A simple life tastes just as good as one that puts on culinary airs.

Honestly, I think that some Christians make a successful prayer life sound like one of Linda's dinner parties. According to their standards, unless you're willing to suffer in the process of prayer, you will never taste and see that the Lord is good. Implied in their complicated instructions is, "I've achieved this, but you probably never will."

Must I park my arthritic knees on a hard floor to get a taste of God? Must I open the windows in winter so I won't fall asleep while praying? Must I dedicate hours shivering on my knees to be invited to God's banquet table? Perhaps on rare occasions it might be a good idea not to be too comfortable, but not as a steady diet. God wants me to come back to his table on a regular basis.

In the parable of the prodigal son, the forgiving father invites his long-lost son to a simple but elegant meal. Within that story is a simple prayer and an answer to prayer as well. What better way to encounter God tonight than to strip down your recipe for prayer to the prodigal's petition, and to receive in response the father's gracious welcoming words?

The Prodigal: "Father, I have sinned against heaven and against you. I am no longer worthy to be called your son" (Luke 15:21).

The Father: "Let's have a feast and celebrate" (Luke 15:23).

 Simplify your thoughts tonight as you repeat, "Taste and see that the LORD is good" (Psalm 34:8).

Day 3:

ST. PATRICK'S BREASTPLATE

Look to your heart, that it be well guarded and defended, that you have a good breastplate for the defense of it.
Samuel Nowell, *Abraham in Arms*

The hymn that follows has become one of my favorites because it gives history and spiritual muscle to living or dying for Christ. I can, for example, imagine Ignatius and Cassie claiming its words for themselves. I heard it first at the ordination of a friend for the Christian ministry. The words are strong armor for any of us who want a heart well guarded and defended so that we can live for Christ.

ST. PATRICK'S BREASTPLATE

I bind unto myself today
The strong Name of the Trinity,
By invocation of the same
The Three in One and One in Three.

I bind this today to me forever
By power of faith, Christ's incarnation;
His baptism in Jordan river,
His death on Cross for my salvation;
His bursting from the spicèd tomb,
His riding up the heavenly way,
His coming at the day of doom
I bind unto myself today.

I bind unto myself the power
Of the great love of cherubim;
The sweet "Well done" in judgment hour,
The service of the seraphim,
Confessors' faith, Apostles' word,
The Patriarchs' prayers, the prophets' scrolls,
All good deeds done unto the Lord
And purity of virgin souls.

I bind unto myself today
The virtues of the star lit heaven,
The glorious sun's life giving ray,
The whiteness of the moon at even,
The flashing of the lightning free,
The whirling wind's tempestuous shocks,
The stable earth, the deep salt sea
Around the old eternal rocks.

I bind unto myself today
The power of God to hold and lead,
His eye to watch, His might to stay,
His ear to hearken to my need.
The wisdom of my God to teach,
His hand to guide, His shield to ward;
The word of God to give me speech,
His heavenly host to be my guard.

❧

Against the demon snares of sin,
The vice that gives temptation force,
The natural lusts that war within,
The hostile men that mar my course;
Or few or many, far or nigh,
In every place and in all hours,
Against their fierce hostility
I bind to me these holy powers.

❧

Against all Satan's spells and whiles,
Against false words of heresy,
Against the knowledge that defiles,
Against the heart's idolatry,
Against the wizard's evil craft,
Against the death wound and the burning,
The choking wave, the poisoned shaft,
Protect me, Christ, till Thy returning.

❧

Christ be with me, Christ within me,
Christ behind me, Christ before me,
Christ beside me, Christ to win me,
Christ to comfort and restore me.
Christ beneath me, Christ above me,
Christ in quiet, Christ in danger,
Christ in hearts of all that love me,
Christ in mouth of friend and stranger.

∼⁀⁀

I bind unto myself the Name,
The strong Name of the Trinity,
By invocation of the same,
The Three in One and One in Three.
By Whom all nature hath creation,
Eternal Father, Spirit, Word:
Praise to the Lord of my salvation,
Salvation is of Christ the Lord.

Cecil Frances Alexander

 As you fall asleep tonight, cross your arms across your chest as you repeat, "Stand firm then . . . with the breastplate of righteousness in place" (Ephesians 6:14).

Day 4:

COMPANY IN THE CLOUDS

Therefore, since we are surrounded by so great a cloud of witnesses, let us also lay aside every weight and the sin that clings so closely, and let us run with perseverance the race that is set before us.

Hebrews 12:1 NRSV

Some years ago in the clouds above a seven-hundred-year-old baroque Austrian town, I beheld an alpine apparition of health and vigor. That day I had planned to treat myself to a panoramic view of Innsbruck, but before I could enjoy the view I had to puff my way uphill to a cable car that would speed me to the top. On the path behind me I heard the brisk footfall of a seasoned hiker. This power-walker possessed far more wind for the work than I did that day.

"Gruß Gott!" ("God's greeting!") called an elderly woman in folk-lore dress. In almost comic contrast to her silver braided hair, lace-trimmed blouse, green print dirndl, and cranberry apron were her mud-brown boots, khaki wool socks, and enormous calf muscles.

Thick veins coursed over her gastrocs like Popeye's spinach-fed biceps. Those robust legs had known a lifetime of marching up that mountain, over eighty years' worth, I reckoned by her wrinkled, smiling face.

It wasn't long before this vision of elderly fitness disappeared from my view. Later, as my cable car lazily ascended up to the Hungerberg station, I caught sight of her again through the clouds, charging up by foot toward the 2,800-foot plateau. The luminescence of her righteous sweat put me to shame. But that old doll in a dirndl had an inner glow of happiness and contentment, the sort of conviction that she would live to be one hundred and love every minute of it.

Why did such a charming sight as Heidi—I had to give her a name in my book of memories—exhaust me? A younger woman of forty-five at the time, I considered packing my hiking boots and heading home to vegetate in front of a fireplace. I even wondered whether I wanted to live into my eighties, much less survive to be a hundred. There are days in my life when I'm not sure that I'll make it through to supper! But Heidi is just the type of company I need in the clouds that surround me. I need friends who can show me how the power of God can sustain me all the days of my life.

Heidi would be almost a hundred years old today. I'll look for her on that mountain the next time I visit Innsbruck. Somehow I know that this spirited old woman in hiking boots is still glowing and growing today as she approaches her centennial mark. And somehow I know that even on the days that Heidi chooses a solitary walk up her beloved mountain, she will never be alone.

Heidi reminds me of a word that the psalmist uses to describe God and his love: *steadfast*. When you're tired and don't want to go on, *steadfast* sounds like intimidation. But when God attends our path, steadfast is just the gift we want—the strength to go on.

May God bring a steadfast friend of your own to your memory tonight and use that friend's example to strengthen and equip you for the race that's before you.

 Imagine yourself and that friend participating in a special activity that you've steadfastly enjoyed all your life as you pray, "Create in me a pure heart, O God, and renew a steadfast spirit within me" (Psalm 51:10).

Day 5:

WORDS FULL OF REST

*"The Lord is my Shepherd" ... links a
lump of common clay to divine destiny.*
Philip Keller, *A Shepherd
Looks at Psalm 23*

A young Japanese pediatrician wrote to me about a case that really bothered him. Hiroshi was no stranger to death, even the death of young children. But this tiny preemie baby really got to him! I know that feeling myself, the unrest of "malignant ifs."

If I were only smarter.

If I had only read one more article.

If I had only stayed up one more hour.

If I had only prayed harder.

If, If, If! But it isn't all up to me and my ifs!

I wrote to Hiroshi and shared stories of my own ifs. They struck a familiar chord with him, but it took him a long time to reply. He was concerned about his imperfect English.

Hiroshi wanted to say it all right. I, for one, am glad that he had to struggle in his heart and not in his head for the words he wanted to say. No American would have said it more beautifully. Hiroshi's words echo Psalm 23, even in the balanced phrases of the Hebrew poetry. "Your words are full of rest," he wrote. "I have got much comfort."

When we link the divine destiny of the Great Shepherd with our common clay story, we too find rest and comfort. No ifs about it!

PSALM 23

The LORD is my shepherd;
    I shall not want.
He maketh me to lie down in green pastures:
    he leadeth me beside the still waters.
He restoreth my soul:
    he leadeth me in the paths of righteousness
    for his name's sake.
Yea, though I walk through the valley of the shadow of death,
    I will fear no evil:
        for thou art with me;
        thy rod and thy staff they comfort me.
Thou preparest a table before me in the presence of mine enemies:
    thou anointest my head with oil;
    my cup runneth over.
Surely goodness and mercy shall follow me all the days of my life:
    and I will dwell in the house of the LORD forever.

KJV

 Instead of reciting your "malignant ifs" tonight, rest in a green pasture by quiet waters as you repeat to yourself, "To the waters of repose he leads me; there he revives my soul" (Psalm 23:2–3 JB).

Day 6:

LET EVENING COME

May my prayer be set before you like incense; may the lifting up of my hands be like the evening sacrifice.

Psalm 141:2

We need more positive images of evening and night if we're going to feel tired, not exhausted. I love Jane Kenyon's poetry, especially this invitation to evening to come on in.

LET EVENING COME

Let the light of late afternoon
shine through chinks in the barn, moving
up the bales as the sun moves down.

❧

Let the cricket take up chafing
as a woman takes up her needles
and her yarn. Let evening come.

❧

Let dew collect on the hoe abandoned

in long grass. Let the stars appear
and the moon disclose her silver horn.

⚬⚬⚬

Let the fox go back to its sandy den.
Let the wind die down. Let the shed
go black inside. Let evening come.

⚬⚬⚬

To the bottle in the ditch, to the scoop
in the oars, to air in the lung
let evening come.

⚬⚬⚬

Let it come, as it will, and don't
be afraid. God does not leave us
comfortless, so let the evening come.

Jane Kenyon[13]

 *Let the evening come to your soul as you repeat,
"Those who enter God's rest also rest from their own
work, just as God did from his" (Hebrews 4:10 RNIV).*

Day 7:

THE SONG OF ZECHARIAH

*Then an angel of the Lord appeared to
[Zechariah], standing at the right
side of the altar of incense.*

Luke 1:11

When the angel took a coal off the altar to touch his lips, Isaiah's tongue was cleansed and loosed into glorious song. Zechariah, on the other hand, would have to wait to sing his canticle because he was so frightened by seeing an angel by his altar.

When fear overwhelmed him, Zechariah didn't believe what Gabriel had to say. As a result, the angel struck him mute until his words were fulfilled. But what a song it was that Zechariah sang when the Holy Spirit loosened the tongue of John the Baptizer's father! As he recovered his speech, Zechariah prophesied about the unique calling of his newborn son.

THE SONG OF ZECHARIAH (BENEDICTUS DOMINUS DEUS)

Praise be to the Lord, the God of Israel,
because he has come and has redeemed his people.

He has raised up a horn of salvation for us
    in the house of his servant David
(as he said through his holy prophets of long ago),
salvation from our enemies
    and from the hand of all who hate us—
to show mercy to our fathers
    and to remember his holy covenant,
    the oath he swore to our father Abraham:
to rescue us from the hand of our enemies,
    and to enable us to serve him without fear
    in holiness and righteousness before him all our days.

And you, my child, will be called a prophet of the Most High;
    for you will go on before the Lord to prepare the way for him,
to give his people the knowledge of salvation
    through the forgiveness of their sins,
because of the tender mercy of our God,
    by which the rising sun will come to us from heaven
to shine on those living in darkness
    and in the shadow of death,
to guide our feet into the path of peace.

Luke 1:68–79

Glory be to the Father, and to the Son,
    and to the Holy Spirit:
As it was in the beginning, is now,
    and will be for ever. Amen.

How did you serve God today? Think about it as you repeat, "Serve him without fear in holiness and righteousness before him all our days" (Luke 1:74–75).

6
SILENT NIGHT

Silence is the element in which great things fashion themselves together.
Maurice Maeterlinck,
The Treasure of the Humble

Day 1:

AN EPIPHANY DREAM

I find my reward in that look in a child's eye which says, "Someone has listened to my story and found it important."

Mary Taylor Previte

Have you ever woken up in the morning and felt that you absolutely had to understand a particular dream? That there was something in your dream that seemed to beg you to follow it the way the wise men followed the star in the East? I felt that way one morning in a hotel room hundreds of miles from home. The dream was so gentle that its very nature seemed to be a promise of safety if I would pursue its meaning.

I was at a place I had known in the past, but it had undergone many changes since my last visit. I walked through a new dining room that had a lot more seats than the one I remembered. I had to go through that dining room to get to the place where I was living. Then I walked back around to the opposite side of the building.

It was dusk and hard to see clearly. On the other side of this dining room was a little sanctuary for a baby bird. Someone whose face I couldn't see pointed the bird out to me. I had to focus hard in those twilight moments to be able to see it, but then I did. The bird was tiny and fragile and blue. The person talking to me suggested that I stick out my finger to see if the bird would hop on it. I did, being careful to be gentle. I didn't want to frighten the baby bird. He hopped on, then hopped off, but the baby bird seemed to trust me.

I wanted to carry that little bird on my finger over to the side of the building where I was staying. The trick would be to keep him on my finger in the dark. If he flew away, he might not be able to find his way back to where he had lived before. Nor had he ever been to the place where I was taking him. I didn't want to cage him up to get him to my place, but there was great risk walking in the dark in the wide open. Would he trust me enough to stay on my finger until we got there or would he fly off? I had to be as gentle as possible if it were to happen. I had to be more gentle than I usually am, but I wanted this baby bird to go with me of his own free will.

Wow, what a dream! I just had to know its meaning. Was I "me" in the dream or a symbol for God? But wasn't God the person talking to me, the one I couldn't see? Despite the challenges in the dream, it offered peaceful feelings. And I loved that fragile little baby bird. If it hadn't been Sunday morning and church time, I would have stayed in my hotel room daydreaming about my night dream.

I got the name of a local church from the hotel concierge and headed that direction. At one intersection I turned right when I should have turned left, but my wrong turn turned out to be God's turn in my day.

During the children's sermon, the pastor called a six-year-old up to the pulpit.

"How big are you?" he asked the child.

"Big enough to hold a bird," the child replied.

I was stunned, and thought about how much better a child can understand how fragile that little bird must be than any adult could.

"I tell you the truth," said Jesus (he always prefaces his remarks that way when he's afraid we won't believe what he's about to say), "anyone who will not receive the kingdom of God like a little child will never enter it" (Luke 18:17). What did God want to teach me about receiving his kingdom?

Last month I fetched a small birdbath and squirrel-proof feeder from a local garden store. Suddenly I am the favorite bird restaurant in the entire neighborhood! And Babu, bless his little Yorkie heart, just sits and watches quietly (except for when he sees wild turkeys from whom he would like a drumstick for dinner).

In the past I have only seen large birds on the trees. Now I'm seeing teeny species checking out this new dining spot. How peaceful it feels to just sit and watch. I don't need to touch or manipulate. My only role here is to support life. That's something that a child—someone without much power—would understand.

The kingdom of God is like that small bluebird. It needs to be received with a gentle hand, the way a child would receive it. Like a Christmas star, it needs to be carried through the darkness from where I find it to where I'm going to live. God's kingdom doesn't need my power to flourish. It simply needs me to gently reach out my hand.

 In the darkness tonight, reach your hand out gently to receive God's kingdom and carry it with you as you repeat, "The unfading beauty of a gentle and quiet spirit . . . is of great worth in God's sight" (1 Peter 3:4).

Day 2:

A CRYING-IN-THE-WILDERNESS PRAYER

To the ill-considered hopes of the last two centuries . . . we can propose only a determined quest for the warm hand of God.
Aleksandr Solzhenitsyn, "Men Have Forgotten God"

Every year during Advent we celebrate the anticipation of Jesus' coming. We rehearse the story, line by line, including the story of his cousin John, who cried in the wilderness to prepare the way of the Lord. To borrow a metaphor from another cranky prophet in the genre of John, each Advent we make a determined quest for the warm hand of God.

I want to say a word here in praise of cranky prophets like John the Baptizer and Aleksandr Solzhenitsyn. It seems to me that we love it when a prophet rails out against the powers and things we consider evil. The Jews of John's time would not have minded if John had pointed to the sins of the Romans. In a similar vein, we in the West sang Solzhenitsyn's praises and awarded him our highest prizes when the Soviets imprisoned him. How clear and brave we found his words when he was speaking about someone else's sins! We couldn't wait until he was liberated so that he could pour out his prophetic words without censorship. Then Solzhenitsyn came to America and was invited to Harvard. And then he really got cranky!

"Destructive and irresponsible freedom has been granted boundless space," the prophet said about our western culture.

"Hastiness and superficiality are the psychic disease of the twentieth century," he declared about our infirmities.

"All the glorified technological achievements of progress . . . do not redeem the twentieth century's moral poverty," he accused our society.[14]

The press tore Solzhenitsyn apart for delivering that message, but they missed a golden opportunity to hear what the prophet was saying. When God offers his warm hand to a man like Solzhenitsyn, he gives him a message that only the humble of heart can hear. The media should have prayed with Solzhenitsyn rather than taking potshots at him from across their desks.

What might the press have heard if they had prayed with this prophet? Here is a prayer that Solzhenitsyn first shared in secret in the gulags and that reached print for the first time in *Vogue* magazine in 1971.

A final note about this prayer. When David Redding asked Solzhenitsyn for permission to quote this prayer in his book *The Prayers I Love*, the "cranky prophet" gave Redding not only permission but also the copyright for the prayer as a gift! As you pray these words with Solzhenitsyn and other readers tonight, think of them as a gift of prayer that you can give to one of your friends.

How simple for me to live with You, O Lord!
How easy to believe in You!

When in confusion, my soul bares itself or bends,
  When the most wise can see no further than this
  night and do not know what the morrow brings;
  You fill me with the clear certainty that
  You exist and that You watch to see that all the
  paths of righteousness be not closed.
From the heights of worldly glory
  I am astonished by the path through despair You
  have provided me
  this path from which I have been worthy enough
  to reflect Your radiance to men.
All that I will yet reflect, You will grant me.
  And for that which I will not succeed in reflecting,
  You have appointed others.
  Amen.

                                   Aleksandr Solzhenitsyn[15]

Be confident tonight that God will watch to see that
all the paths of righteousness are open to you as
you repeat, "Thanks be to God for his indescribable
gift! (2 Corinthians 9:15).

Day 3:

WHAT CAN I GIVE HIM?

It's a wonderful story and you want to be part of it.
Garrison Keillor, in a monologue about
Christmas in Lake Wobegon

Thanksgiving weekend I discovered a most startling artistic treatment of the Christmas story. My sister and I had the privilege of visiting Jane Higgins in her Gainesville, New York, studio (and sharing a generous bowl of her husband's chicken noodle soup). Jane's favorite medium is collage. Not only does she cut and paste from a wide variety of clippings, she also digs into her rich knowledge of literature and history to enrich the images she chooses. When I spotted her new work "Gift of the Medics," my first reaction was, "Whoa!" Jane herself admits she was concerned that her modern interpretation of the Christmas story might be considered sacrilegious by some. But then I studied the piece more closely.

The Holy Family is there in classical Italian representation. Mary and Joseph bend attentively over the cot that bears the Christ child. But instead of a manger for a cradle, Jesus is resting on an ambulance gurney, surrounded by EMTs. The wise men attend as well, one with a stethoscope draped around his robes. Their gifts stacked before the Holy Child: over-the-counter and prescription medications. The communion of saints attends as well, one holding the bag of IV fluids that flow into his veins. Ambulance attendants focus on their rescue task and draw our eyes into the van they will use to transport their patient, its walls covered with the starry cosmos.

"What gift can I bring you, poor as I am?" wrote Christina Rossetti in her Christmas hymn *In a Bleak Midwinter.* Who am I to bring God a gift, poor in spirit as I am? Who am I to paint the "profanity" of my daily work into this picture? I drove back home that Sunday planning to make it to my church on time to share this painting, which I had bought, with the folks there. Quite a crowd gathered. Everyone was excited. And each one had an opinion.

"I see it as breathing life into the church," said Nancy, who heads our Healing the Whole Person ministry.

"It reminds me of the Scripture 'Inasmuch as you have done it to the least of these my brethren, you've done it to me' (Matthew 25:40)," added Randy, our youth minister.

As we read Rossetti's lovely words tonight, may we be as humble as the shepherds and as bold as the wise men. Let us consider what gift we can bring the Child because the story is so wonderful that we want and need to be a part of it.

IN THE BLEAK MIDWINTER

In the bleak midwinter, frosty wind made moan,
Earth stood hard as iron, water like a stone;
Snow had fallen, snow on snow, snow on snow,
In the bleak midwinter, long ago.

❧

Our God, heaven cannot hold him, nor earth sustain;
Heaven and earth shall flee away when he comes to reign.

In the bleak midwinter a stable place sufficed
The Lord God Almighty, Jesus Christ.

❧

Angels and archangels may have gathered there,
Cherubim and seraphim thronged the air;
But his mother only, in her maiden bliss,
Worshiped the beloved with a kiss.

❧

What can I give him, poor as I am?
If I were a shepherd, I would bring a lamb;
If I were a Wise Man, I would do my part;
Yet what I can I give him: give my heart.

Christina G. Rossetti

As you fall asleep tonight, picture yourself at the manger on that bleak, midwinter first Christmas night. As you behold the mystery of Christ's coming, repeat: "Every good and perfect gift is from above, coming down from the Father of the heavenly lights" (James 1:17).

Day 4:

LAURA, THE WHITE HOUSE ANGEL

Our Lord comforts a soul with angels' song.

Walter Hilton, *The Song of Angels*

"Fear not!" That's how angels always introduce themselves when a baby is about to be born. Without those angel whispers, how would parents ever have the courage to bring new life into this crazy world? Some would call Laura's parents crazy for even thinking of bringing her into this world.

Laura's mother, Joan, is so skilled a crafter of the old American art form of wheat weaving that the White House staff invited her to make an angel ornament for the East Wing Christmas tree. With great love Joan formed wee wheaten hands to hold a golden trumpet. She shaped a little halo to crown the tiny head. When her task was complete, Joan smiled to herself, perhaps because this angel was the finest little woven wheat sculpture that she had ever created. Finally Joan gave a name to her angel: Laura. That special name was the most perfect part of a job well done.

I'm sure that the First Family noticed "Laura" there on the Christmas tree. Although successful contenders of other angel artisans surrounded Laura, angels on a mission stick out even in an angel crowd. But did the First Family ever learn that blessed angel's name, or realize that Laura had taken part in a miraculous story?

I was working in my lab at Yale when Joan drew me into the story. A colleague at Johns Hopkins had given her my name. Somehow Joan hoped that the research I was doing could help the baby she carried in her womb. She told me about all her children—one on earth and two in heaven. A one-in-a-million rare disease with a very long name had taken her babies. If it happens once in a family, the chances are one in four that it will happen again. Joan and Joe had lost two times out of three, and now they were pregnant again.

"Is there any test yet to diagnose FHL* prior to birth?" Joan asked. They hoped that treatment could be started earlier than was possible with Michael and Jeffrey. I didn't have any answers. Like Joan, I only had hope.

"Have you ever looked at the placenta in this disease?" Joan asked me. "Or studied blood from the umbilical cord?"

I tried not to sound patronizing when I told her that there was no value in looking at these tissues. FHL does not affect newborns. It typically takes at least six weeks of life for the disease to show up. An FHL baby had to experience life before things started to go wrong.

When Laura was born, Joan and Joe knew right away that she had the disease. And they knew that Laura was too sick for treatment to save her life. But it was late on Friday afternoon! Joan and Joe knew what hospitals are like on weekends. If they didn't act fast, the samples they wanted me to test might be forever lost.

On Monday morning, the samples were in my lab. I remembered what I had told Joan: "FHL doesn't happen to newborns." And yet it

---

*FHL is an abbreviation for Familial Hemophagocytic Lymphohistiocytosis.

did this time. How could a mother's instincts be more accurate than my medical knowledge? I suspect there was a whole heavenly host of angels standing there laughing at me that day. Not only was the test positive, but it showed higher levels for the FHL substance than any other disease known to humankind. And the very fact that it was elevated opened up important clues to the nature of the disease. Today we understand far better what goes wrong and why.

Her mother held sweet little Laura safely in her arms until the baby took her flight home to Jesus. Joan thought that she was like a little angel, but angels don't go to all this trouble to tell a story without another one to follow. Laura was still in my heart a year later when another beloved baby waltzed into my life.

The first time I met Katherine, I nicknamed her my little Crumb Bunny. She was critically ill when I first met her and her parents, Barry and Sue. If it hadn't been for Laura, I might not have pieced the puzzle together in time.

They had lost another child before her.

It was such a shock to lose Ryan that Barry and Sue agreed to an autopsy.

"It looks like an overwhelming infection," the doctors said when it was all over. "It shouldn't happen again." If it hadn't been for Laura, I might have agreed with them. Was it possible that Ryan had died of FHL and not the infection they had reported?

While Sue stayed with Crumb Bunny at the hospital, Barry drove to Ryan's doctors and picked up the autopsy slides. The telltale cells were there, but no one had noticed them. Because Ryan's doctors hadn't thought about FHL, they had missed it!

Thanks to her brother Ryan, Crumb Bunny's diagnosis was now established. The diagnosis may have taken a week, but the search for a donor lasted for a long and agonizing year. Finally we heard from a

British bone marrow registry that they had a donor. The certain knowledge that Crumb Bunny would not survive without this procedure was encouragement enough to proceed.

When I say that every aspect of the transplant went smoothly and without major complication, I am not exaggerating. Perhaps the trickiest—if not most impossible—task was to keep the baby in the special isolation room without a door. Crumb Bunny was only seventeen months old at the time. How could we expect a baby to understand and obey the illogical rule not to go through an open door? Somehow she did until it was time to go home. And then the Crumb Bunny was on the move! Today Katherine is nine years old. When she first started school, she called herself a friend of God.

God really needed a good friend when the next family came along. Fortunately, Crumb Bunny's mother heard about their story. As clinical narratives go, Chase and Tyler's short lives are recorded in gentler terms than typical, terse, just-the-facts-ma'am medical prose. Like Dr. Luke, whose Gospel charted holy pregnancies in rich detail, Chase and Tyler's doctors noted the following important facts about this little family:

"The parents wished to take Chase home to be with them until her death at home."

"Tyler was taken to his mother's room to spend the remaining time of his life with his parents and his sister."

My own role in the next part of the story is pitifully small. Crumb Bunny's mother had given Christie my name. I coached her on how to find an obstetrician who would listen to a mother.

Christie felt fine until the sixth month of her pregnancy. When the fetal movements stopped, she went in for an ultrasound to see what was happening. Christie's heart raced when she saw the swollen liver and spleen on the ultrasound screen. Just as with her first two

FHL babies, this little tummy was tense with fluid. Powerless to help his wife, Randy saw the tears forming in Christie's eyes. He felt the life of his little son ebbing away, along with his own strength.

"We have a suggestion to make," the obstetrician said. "We're willing to try something to see if we can carry him through till he's old enough to be born."

Christie and Randy listened to an amazing but potentially dangerous plan. Chemotherapy could be given into the umbilical vein. No, it had never been done before. Yes, Christie herself might experience side effects. But all she could hear was that her baby might live. They could even get a sample for the bone marrow type while they were at it. The plan made great sense!

It was like a miracle to watch the next ultrasound, but Christie already knew what it would show. Andrew (they had already named him) was kicking her again, as if to say, "Good going, Mom! That was a super idea!" Within three weeks, the kicking stopped again. Once more the liver and spleen had swelled up. Another treatment, another success. This time Christie vomited after the treatment, and her hair began to thin. But the two treatments added six whole weeks of safety, and the doctors already knew what type of donor to look for.

Andrew weighed a whopping five pounds eight ounces when he was born. He got his next dose of treatment as soon as he was out in the world. And at six months of age he had his bone marrow transplant. Today he's reached the ripe old age of five.

As I think about Andrew's story, I hear echoes of Joan's original question as if some angel were whispering in my ear. "Is there any test yet to diagnose an FHL baby prior to birth?" And her idea about research. "Have you ever looked at the placenta? Or studied the blood from the umbilical cord?" That's why doctors need angels too.

When we're afraid to look foolish to our colleagues, doctors need to hear a rousing "Fear not!" When we're afraid to try something new because we might fail, we need an angel to trumpet loudly again, "Fear not!" And when a mom or dad says, "Have you ever thought of . . ." we need not fear, because God will choose the angelically foolish things of the world to confound those who think they are wise. *Glory to God in the highest! And on earth deep peace and good will.*

 No matter what you fear, hear the angel's message tonight. And believe God's promise: "Fear not, for I have redeemed you; I have summoned you by name; you are mine" (Isaiah 43:1).

Day 5:

YOU ARE MY SON

Of the Father's love begotten ere the worlds began to be, he is Alpha and Omega, he the source, the ending he of the things that are, that have been and that future years shall see, evermore and evermore.

Aurelius Clemens Prudentius

One of my favorite childhood Christmas memories is of watching (as well as hearing) our church's rather large basso profundo sing his portions of Handel's *Messiah*. As the nations so furiously raged together, he and his many chins shook like a bowlful of jelly.

Here's a suggestion for a home Bible study for the next Christmas season. Take a score of the *Messiah* and find the Scripture texts on which the Christmas portions of the oratorio were based. During the four weeks of Advent, invite your friends and neighbors to a "*Messiah* listen-in" at your home. Make an Advent wreath with four candles for the four weeks of Advent. Each week as you light the candles, play a recording of the portion of the *Messiah* that you'll be studying that evening. Explore the messianic meaning of Handel's chosen texts with your guests.

You might want to light a candle yourself tonight as we read Psalm 2. See if you can spot the arias and choruses from the *Messiah* imbedded within it.

PSALM 2

Why do the nations conspire
    and the peoples plot in vain?
The kings of the earth take their stand
    and the rulers gather together
against the LORD
    and against his Anointed One.
"Let us break their chains," they say,
    "and throw off their fetters."

❮❯

The One enthroned in heaven laughs;
    the Lord scoffs at them.
Then he rebukes them in his anger
    and terrifies them in his wrath, saying,
"I have installed my King
    on Zion, my holy hill."

❮❯

I will proclaim the decree of the LORD:

❮❯

He said to me, "You are my Son;
    today I have become your Father.
Ask of me,
    and I will make the nations your inheritance,

the ends of the earth your possession.
You will rule them with an iron scepter;
    you will dash them to pieces like pottery."

                  ❧

Therefore, you kings, be wise;
    be warned, you rulers of the earth.
Serve the LORD with fear
    and rejoice with trembling.
Kiss the Son, lest he be angry
    and you be destroyed in your way,
for his wrath can flare up in a moment.
    Blessed are all who take refuge in him.

Share the Father's delight tonight as you behold Jesus and hear the Father's words: "This is my Son, whom I love; with him I am well pleased" (Matthew 3:17).

Day 6:

THE OTHER GRANDMOTHER

Had Mary been filled with reason,
there'd have been no room for the child.
Madeleine L'Engle, "After Annunciation"

Someday in heaven I want to chat with a long list of supporting actors and actresses in the biblical drama whose detailed stories are as yet unpublished.

Take Simon Peter's wife, for example. We've met her mother, even taken the woman's temperature and felt her pulse in Scripture. But what of the long-suffering woman who was married to that impulsive fisherman? I suspect all of eternity will not be enough for her to spin all her fisher's-wife tales.

And then there's Pharaoh's daughter. We don't even know her name. No one knew better than she what her father did to those who disobeyed his commands. The first time she saw the wet nurse Miriam brought to nurse young Moses, did she suspect it was the child's own mother? Or was her faith so strong that she hoped that was just who would show up to nanny her adopted son? I hope to have the chance to chat with her someday.

And what of Joseph's mother? Again, we don't even know her name. What an unusual position she was in. Did she notice Mary's waist thickening too soon after the wedding? Did she take her son aside and grill him about what had happened?

Kathy Coffey invites us to share the sacred moment when Joseph's mother first held Jesus in her arms.

THE OTHER GRANDMOTHER

What of Joseph's mother?
Unstoried and unsung,
did she question the
poignant girl, and
hunt her son's resemblance
in the mysterious child?

❧

Or did she, like others in the story,
build from doubt a ladder to delight
in a newborn fist and wobbly head?
She didn't guess that God
might clothe himself in skin,
or stir at her whisper, "grandson."

Kathy Coffey[16]

 Use a lullaby tune to sing yourself to sleep with the words, "For nothing is impossible with God" (Luke 1:37).

Day 7:

THE SONG OF SIMEON

Simeon ... was waiting for the conso-
lation of Israel, and the Holy Spirit
was upon him.

Luke 2:25

Of the four Gospels, only Luke's Christmas story includes a set of priceless canticles that surrounded the Savior's birth. In contrast to the angel's visitation to Zechariah, a priest, the Holy Spirit pays a visit to a layman in the Song of Simeon.

For his entire life, Simeon had looked forward to the coming of the Promised One, whom he called "Israel's consolation." As a reward for his faithfulness, God promised Simeon that he would not taste death until he saw the Lord's Messiah.

As you read Simeon's song, imagine what it would have been like to live your life in holy anticipation and finally be there in the temple to take that baby in your arms, knowing exactly who he was.

THE SONG OF SIMEON (NUNC DIMITTIS)

Sovereign Lord, as you have promised,
   you now dismiss your servant in peace.
For my eyes have seen your salvation,

which you have prepared in the sight of all people,
a light for revelation to the Gentiles,
    and for glory to your people Israel.

Luke 2:29–32

Glory be to the Father, and to the Son,
    and to the Holy Spirit:
As it was in the beginning, is now,
    and will be for ever. Amen.

 As God "dismisses" you from wakefulness tonight,
as his servant, take that babe into your arms and
heart as you repeat, "Sovereign Lord, as you have
promised, you now dismiss your servant in peace"
(Luke 2:29).

7

RISEN WITH HEALING IN HIS WINGS

Mild he lays his glory by, born that man no more may die.

Charles Wesley

Day 1:

HEALING A NIGHTMARE

Dreams don't make you a better person.
It's what you do with them that counts.
Ann Spangler, *Dreams and Miracles*

About three months after the first Boeing 747 jumbo jets first started flying the transatlantic routes, I was scheduled to fly to Europe for the first time. As excited as I was by the adventure, I was a bit concerned by magazine reports of nuts and bolts coming loose in the engines. If the pilot heard funny noises in the engines, an article reported, he was instructed to land immediately. Now how do you do that in the middle of the Atlantic?

My flight was scheduled to leave Kennedy Airport at 7 P.M., but at 9 P.M. we were still in the passenger lounge. No explanations, only apologies, were offered for the delay. Finally we were allowed to board, but the plane did not immediately taxi to the runway. About the time free drinks were served, we passengers became suspicious. Then the captain's voice came over the PA system.

"Sorry for the delay, folks, but we have a little problem we're still working on."

Nuts-and-bolts type of problem? I wondered.

"One of the lights is out on our right wing. The chief mechanic is on his way from home to repair it."

Yeah, sure. Likely story!

"He's stuck in traffic on the Long Island Expressway. Sit back and relax. As soon as that old bulb is changed, we'll take off."

Time passed. Dinner was served. And another round of free drinks was offered. Then came the film, but there was a little problem with that as well. The video was functioning, but the audio was out. Just about the time the pilot announced our takeoff, Gregory Peck came on the screen with furrowed brow in *Marooned*. We were watching the story of a malfunctioning spacecraft lost in space, silently circling the earth.

My spacecraft landed safely in London, and I looked forward to a few hours' sleep at the hotel. Sometime during that nap, I had a dream that has been with me since childhood. Long before NASA started the space race, I would dream of circling the earth in a narrow vessel of metal and glass. Sometimes my head was stuck out into space, as if protruding from a turtle shell. In other scenes my head was inside my orbiting coffin. I woke up in a strange bed, gasping for breath. But finally I remembered when I first began dreaming that dream.

I was eight years old during the great polio epidemic of 1948. In those days polio, not cancer, was every parent's worst nightmare. Even comic books warned children about the dreaded disease. I put away my favorite dolls, Raggedy Ann and Andy, when they posed next to an iron lung, begging for a cure ten cents at a time. Even Hollywood reflected the great fear of that age. In one film, a villain pulled the plug on the helpless victim's respirator. In another, the heroine was in peril during an electrical storm. When the lights flickered, her iron lung faltered. These stories took my breath away, and translated my fear into a dream. In London that morning, with measured breaths, I announced to myself, "Now I understand. End of the fear." At least, that's what I thought.

A few years ago I had to have a brain MRI in my own hospital. I order so many of these tests for my patients that I'm well-known in that department. I joked with the technicians until they rolled my head under the magnet. Suddenly I gasped for breath. This felt too much like my old feared nightmare. Worse yet, my head was inside the tight-fitting turtle shell rather than sticking out. I began to panic. The only thing that saved me from screaming to get out of there and abort the test was that the staff all knew me. I would have been embarrassed to admit my fear.

I tried to explain the origin of my fear to myself, but that didn't work. Then I closed my eyes and invited Jesus in, into that confined space that I feared, into the feelings of that old dream. In that prayer, he took my hand. He breathed life into the air around me and pushed back the walls that confined me. He stayed with me until the test was complete.

The healing peace that Jesus gives is more than the absence of fear. His peace is his presence, an active force. More important than understanding the origin of our fears, more powerful than unearthing our feelings about our fears, is the presence of God in those nightmarish moments.

 As you fall asleep tonight, invite Jesus into a situation you fear as you repeat, "Surely I am with you always" (Matthew 28:20).

Day 2:

ANSWERED PRAYER

The wish to pray is a prayer in itself.
George Bernanos, *Diary of*
a Country Priest

A friend wrote me some really good news about his wife: "Jill learned last week that all her lupus tests are coming up negative. [Her doctor] has declared her in official remission. We are grateful. She still maintains the healthy lifestyle that probably helped get her where she is, but, thanks be to God for his mercy—the first remission in fourteen years!"

If you read *Breakfast for the Heart*, you already know Jill. In a chapter titled "A Jaw Breaker for Death," I used her story and those of a few other friends to illustrate how we can pray for healing by substituting the names of diseases for the places where the psalmists had used the words *enemy* and *foe*. This is what I prayed for Jill:

"When lupus advances against Jill to devour her kidneys, when her lymphocytes attack her, they will stumble and fall" (Psalm 27:2).

Well, lupus and those overactive lymphocytes have stumbled and fallen indeed! But when I wrote those words in *Breakfast*, did I really believe that God would answer my prayer for Jill? Encouraged by her remission and wondering about other possibly answered prayers, I browsed through the stories of the other four friends I had written about in that piece.

"Who rises up for LaRee against the wicked tumor? Who stands up for LaRee against the evil cells? The Lord our God will wipe them out" (Psalm 94:16, 23).

During her hospitalization for surgery, former San Francisco Giants baseball star Dave Dravecky called LaRee. Dave, who lost his pitching arm to the same form of cancer that was rising up against LaRee, calls himself an "encourager" these days. Great job description, Dave! And good work, fella! More than four years have passed since LaRee's surgery and radiation and Dave's encouraging prayer. The wicked tumor has not been seen since.

"You exalted Jen above the breast cancer; from violent effects of chemotherapy you rescued her" (Psalm 18:48).

Jen is a doctor who had to learn firsthand what it means to be a patient. She has finished her treatment now and has returned to the family practice she loves. "This may sound weird," Jen comments, "but thank God for cancer!" Dr. Jen notices how much better a listener she is these days. She has much more to offer her patients than she had before she shared their experience.

"Carl's arthritis will be ashamed and dismayed; it will turn back in sudden disgrace" (Psalm 6:10).

Thanks to two new hip joints, old Carl is springing around like a young billy goat these days. He's especially grateful that he has the mobility to help his wife, Nancy, subject of the next psalm-prayer request:

"How long must Nancy wrestle with her thoughts and every day have sorrow in her heart? How long will the Alzheimer's triumph over her?" (Psalm 13:2).

With her husband's encouragement, Nancy participated in a research trial for a new drug for Alzheimer's disease. Since she started on this medication, Nancy has suffered no further memory loss. In fact, so many Alzheimer's patients have benefited from the drug that the FDA has approved it for wider use.

It pays to write down our prayer requests. Not only does a prayer journal remind us to pray again for friends, but it also brings the answers to prayers to the forefront of our hearts.

I knew you would be encouraged by these five short stories of answered prayer, so I asked each of these friends this question: "If you knew the whole world was praying for you, what one prayer request would you make?" Pray for:

> Carl and Nancy, that they will be able to live out the rest of their lives in their own home.
>
> Jen, that she will have the strength and courage to faithfully care for a young mother in her practice who is dying of breast cancer.
>
> LaRee's friend Jim, who needs to know that God loves him beyond anything he can imagine.
>
> Jill's wonderful kids, that they will continue to grow in their Christian faith.

Won't you pray along with my friends? Remember that they're counting on you! I promise to keep you posted.

 As you pray for your own friends and mine tonight, affirm that "I will come and proclaim your mighty acts, O Sovereign LORD . . . to this day I declare your marvelous deeds" (Psalm 71:16–17).

Day 3:

HAIL THEE, FESTIVAL DAY

I dropped the ointments. I crept forward and went down on my knees and looked inside—
> Walter Wangerin Jr., *Reliving the Passion: Meditations on the Suffering, Death and Resurrection of Jesus as Recorded in Mark*

Some church musicians suggest that the glorious Easter hymn that follows is too complex musically to entrust to congregational singing. They recommend that only a trained choir be allowed to sing it. What a cheat! While I admit that it's metrically tricky, it's such a treat to sing that it's worth taking the risk that the congregation will mess with the metrics. In my church we sing "Hail Thee, Festival Day" every Easter Sunday as the recessional hymn. It's common to see folks in the congregation huddling together in clustered quartets and quintets to help each other find their way through. If you've never heard this wonderful hymn before, you can listen to it on the Internet at the Cyber Hymnal: http://www.tch.simplenet.com/htm/h/hailthee.htm.

(But since you promised me you were going to turn off your computer before going to bed, you'll have to wait for the morning!)

HAIL THEE, FESTIVAL DAY

Easter:
> Refrain: Hail thee, festival day! Blest day to be hallowed forever,
> Day when our Lord was raised, breaking the kingdom of death.

⋘⋙

> All the fair beauty of earth, from the death of the winter arising!
> Every good gift of the year now with its Master returns.
> Rise from the grave now, O Lord, the author of life and creation,
> Treading the pathway of death, new life you give to us all.

⋘⋙

Ascension:
> Refrain: Hail thee, festival day! Blest day to be hallowed forever,
> Day when our risen Lord rose in the heavens to reign.

⋘⋙

> He who was nailed to the cross is Ruler and Lord of all people.
> All things created on earth sing to the glory of God.
> Daily the loveliness grows, adorned with glory of blossom;
> Heaven her gates unbars, flinging her increase of light.

⋘⋙

Pentecost:
> Refrain: Hail thee, festival day! Blest day to be hallowed forever,
> Day when the Holy Ghost shone in the world full of grace.

Bright and in likeness of fire, on those who await your appearing
You whom the Lord had foretold suddenly, swiftly descend.
Forth from the Father you come with sevenfold mystical offering,
Pouring on all human souls infinite riches of God.

All Occasions:
Refrain: Hail thee, festival day! Blest day to be hallowed forever,
Day when our Lord was raised, breaking the kingdom of death.

God the Almighty, the Lord, the Ruler of earth and the heavens,
Guard us from harm without; cleanse us from evil within;
Jesus, the health of the world, enlighten our minds,
     great Redeemer,
Son of the Father supreme, only begotten of God.
Spirit of life and of power, now flow in us, fount of our being,
Light that enlightens us all, life that in all may abide.
Praise to the giver of good! O lover and author of concord,
Pour out your balm on our days; order our ways in your peace.

Venatius Honorius Fortunatus

 Refreshed by this lovely hymn, fall asleep with these words on your lips tonight: "Since, then, you have been raised with Christ, set your hearts on things above, where Christ is seated at the right hand of God" (Colossians 3:1).

Day 4:

RESURRECTION POWER

*The idea of the resurrection of the body
affirms our connectedness with nature
. . . the hope of the resurrection means
that our place in nature is not a prison
sentence but fully God's intention.*
A. J. Conyers, *The Renewal of All Things*

"We're supposed to pass through the valley of the shadow of death, not camp out there," said Senator Max Cleland. If anyone would be able to picture the shadowy valley, it would be Max. Army Major Maury Cralle was there in Vietnam when a grenade blew off both of Max's legs and one of his arms. Major Cralle recalls his own response to the young soldier's plight: "Geez, it's a shame [Cleland] wasn't just killed."

One ethicist commenting on euthanasia imagined a case of suffering so horrendous that he would hope he himself would have the courage to kill for mercy, a case remarkably similar to Cleland's. He described a wounded soldier in Vietnam who lost all four limbs from a land mine and was reduced "to a trunk attached to a face transfixed in horror."

Max Cleland can relate to that picture. He survived Vietnam, but on his first trip outside Walter Reed Army Hospital, he fell out of his wheelchair into the gutter. When he looked up, Cleland saw "horrified faces of onlookers frozen in shock." He describes himself like a "fish flopping on a riverbank."

Although that's a horrible picture, a physical torture that rivals crucifixion, Cleland looks back on that time as a necessary prelude to a far better future. "Without a crucifixion, there would be no resurrection." Before we can be raised with Christ, we must die to our dreams. God has better ones to take their place.

None of Cleland's shocked onlookers at Walter Reed took his life in the name of mercy. At age twenty-six, he became the youngest state senator ever elected in Georgia. Later, under President Carter, he served as chief of the Veterans Administration, where he was a vigorous advocate for the rights of the disabled. Today he serves as a United States senator from Georgia.

Every year Max celebrates his annual "Alive Day" with old comrades. On one of those occasions Major Cralle was there and admitted, "I thought you were dead" to the man he once thought would have been better off that way. They stood together under a banner that proclaimed: "We're glad you're alive."

It takes courage to find and name your power word. Sometimes we must visit the valley of shadows to even give our hope a name.

No matter what weakness you feel in your life tonight, feel the power of the risen Christ as you repeat, "I want to know Christ and the power of his resurrection" (Philippians 3:10).

Day 5:

THE FIRST DAY OF THE WEEK

I have concluded that going to church is an unnatural activity. It does not make sense. . . . Still we go. . . . No matter where my job took me, the church was always there.
Lyn Cryderman, *Glory Land: A Memoir of a Lifetime in Church*

Sunday mornings eight-year-old Rebecca wiggles in a front-row pew of Grace Church in Trumbull, Connecticut. She and her mom, our pastor's wife, sit two pews in front of where I usually park. Sometimes I wonder if Grace's residential PK (pastor's kid) sees church life differently than those of us who volunteer to come each Sunday.

Rather than remain pewbound, Rebecca sinks to her knees with her back to her father up front in the pulpit. Using the pew seat as a writing desk, Rebecca's stylus fills a magic silver slate. As my middle-aged vibrato breaks in mid-hymnody, Rebecca looks up from her work and stares me down with a semi-toothless grin. Then her eyes drop back down as she scribbles furiously. If you want to know my opinion, Rebecca is writing a book like one I read recently called *Glory Land: A Memoir of a Lifetime in Church.*

Glory Land author Lyn Cryderman grew up in a front pew like Rebecca. As a young PK, Lyn set his sights on all the amusing church mice he came to love as an extended family. Come on now, fellow pew mice, you've got to admit that we can be mighty amusing, especially from a little child's point of view. When I read Lyn's playful sacred diary, I felt very much at home. He reminded me of a verse in the Psalms I learned as a very young child: "I was glad when they said unto me, 'Let us go into the house of the LORD'" (Psalm 122:1 KJV).

The story of another PK comes to mind when I think about glad-in-the-house Sundays. Another pewbound pastor's kid, Walter Wangerin Jr., contemplated the deep mysteries of the faith every Sunday. If the church was indeed the "house of the Lord," where in his house did the Lord actually live? Walter shares his wondering, wiggling explorations in a delightful essay, "Looking for Jesus in All the Wrong Places."

At every possible opportunity, young Wally slipped out from under his mother's watchful eye to investigate yet another candidate for the spot where the Lord lived in the church his father pastored. Each time he explored, he was disappointed that he didn't find the Lord where he expected to find him. Finally his three-year-old little boy's mind clicked onto the most mysterious location that he knew of in the church. Surely that must be where the Lord lives! When his mother wasn't looking, Wally made his way for that awesome place where very possibly Jesus lived. You and I know that location as the ladies' room.

Wally may not have found Jesus in the powder room, but he did discover a longing in his heart to be in God's house and to search him out with all diligence. I'm grateful to Walter and Lyn and Rebecca for all their wiggling explorations. Some Sundays I too need to wiggle out of the order of worship to contemplate deep spiritual mysteries. This morning, as we read Psalm 122 in unison at Grace Church, I give myself permission to meditate on how good it is just to be here in the Lord's house.

Where do I find Jesus in Grace Church this morning? Okay, he is represented in the stunning stained-glass window where he serves the Last Supper to his disciples. And he is here at Holy Communion when he invites us to take and eat and remember him. But most of all I find Jesus in the hearts of his people.

My friend Jane reads the Old Testament lesson this morning. Jane and I have been pals since college days, but I'm still awestruck by the way she glows when she reads Scripture, and by the way she holds the Bible high when she finishes the lesson to say, "This is the Word of the Lord!"

Jane's husband is our official church greeter. Every congregation needs someone like Norbert (who has never met a pun he doesn't adore). When Norbert says, "Welcome to Grace Church!" you know that you are welcome here.

We have two little altar girls today facing each other like matched candlesticks as the pastor reads the gospel lesson. Laura and Olivia are glad to be there with us, doing their part. I hope they know where the Lord is this morning, because I surely do. Their mom and dad love Jesus with all their heart, mind, soul, and strength. These sweet pre-ladies only need look at their mom and dad to find the Savior in our church.

When I look into the hearts of each of these saints this morning, I find Jesus. Best of all, Jesus is in all the right places. "I was glad when they said unto me, 'Let us go into the house of the Lord.'" This verse is my memoir of my lifetime in church.

PSALM 122

I was glad when they said to me,
    "Let us go to the house of the LORD!"
Our feet are standing
    within your gates, O Jerusalem.

Jerusalem—built as a city
    that is bound firmly together.
To it the tribes go up,
    the tribes of the LORD,
as was decreed for Israel,
    to give thanks to the name of the LORD.

For there the thrones for judgment were set up,
    the thrones of the house of David.
Pray for the peace of Jerusalem:
    "May they prosper who love you.
Peace be within your walls,
    and security within your towers."
For the sake of my relatives and friends,
    I will say, "Peace be within you."
For the sake of the house of the LORD our God,
    I will seek your good.

NRSV

Think about last Sunday and where you saw the Lord in his house as you repeat, "I was glad when they said unto me, 'Let us go to the house of the LORD'" (Psalm 122:1 NRSV).

Day 6:

EASTER WINGS

The angel rolled the stone away on Easter morning, on Easter morning.

A spiritual

George Herbert, a great hymn writer, was also an accomplished poet whose gifts extended to the visual realm. When the text of this poem is properly aligned, you can see the angels who will roll the stone away from Jesus' tomb.

EASTER WINGS

Lord, who createdst man in wealth and store,
Though foolishly he lost the same,
Decaying more and more
Till he became
Most poor:
With thee
O let me rise
As larks, harmoniously,
And sing this day Thy victories:
Then shall the fall further the flight in me.
My tender age in sorrow did begin:
And still with sicknesses and shame

Thou didst so punish sin,
That I became
Most thin.
With thee
Let me combine
And feel this day thy victory:
For, if I imp my wing on thine,
Affliction shall advance the flight in me.

George Herbert

As you fall asleep tonight, celebrate Jesus' promise: "I am the resurrection and the life. Those who believe in me will live, even though they die will live, and everyone who believes in me will never die" (John 11:25 NRSV).

Day 7:

A SONG TO THE LAMB

Whether I was in the body or out of the body when I wrote it I do not know. I did think I did see all Heaven before me, and the great God Himself.
George Frederick Handel

When in my "life sentence" to church did I first see all heaven before me? Perhaps it was the first time I heard Handel's *Messiah* from the vantage point of the Cherub Choir.

Robed in red, decked out in white surplice, my twin sister and I joined the youngest choristers at the early age of three. How wonderful to stand in front of the congregation and be such an important part of the life of the church! We got to stand while the congregation sat. But there was one song that brought the congregation to its feet while the choir was singing.

The first time I heard the senior choir sing the "Hallelujah Chorus," I didn't understand the great mystery that brought everyone to their feet. I remember someone saying, "This is the Christian's national anthem," but it was many years later that I learned what happened the first time an audience heard the song.

The King of England wanted to hear Handel's newest musical work. When the choir got to the "Hallelujah Chorus," the music was so glorious that the king rose to his feet. Following his lead, his subjects rose as well. Since then, all audiences have followed that custom. We rise in astonishment. We stand in respect. When we hear the "Hallelujah Chorus" today, the Holy Spirit breaks into our midst the same way he visited the composer as he tried to finish this most beloved piece of music in the history of the human race.

For days Handel had not touched any of the food his servant had brought him. Then one day his servant found him weeping in his room, stretched over his work. Handel had just completed setting two texts from John's book of Revelation to music. When the "Hallelujah Chorus" was complete, Handel exclaimed, "Whether I was in the body or out of the body when I wrote it I do not know. I did think I did see all Heaven before me, and the great God Himself."

Tonight as we recite the Song of the Lamb, let us close with the words of Handel's beautiful and truly inspired "Hallelujah Chorus." It is indeed a glorious amen to our everlasting life sentence.

A Song to the Lamb (Dignus es)

You are worthy, our Lord and God,
    to receive glory and honor and power,
for you created all things,
    and by your will they were created
    and have their being. . . .

❧

Because you were slain,
    and with your blood you purchased men for God,
    from every tribe and language and people and nation.
You have made them to be a kingdom and priests to serve our God. . . .

To him who sits on the throne and to the Lamb,
be praise and honor and glory and power,
for ever and ever!

Revelation 4:11; 5:9–10, 13

*Glory be to the Father, and to the Son,
and to the Holy Spirit:
As it was in the beginning, is now,
and will be for ever. Amen.*

Hallelujah! Hallelujah! For the Lord God omnipotent reigneth.
And he shall reign forever and ever.
King of kings, forever and ever.
Lord of lords, hallelujah, hallelujah.

*The "Hallelujah Chorus," adapted
from Revelation 19:6; 11:15*

 *Use every inch of your holy imagination to visu-
alize God's throne room as you repeat, "To him
who sits on the throne and to the Lamb be praise
and honor and glory and power, for ever and
ever!" (Revelation 5:13).*

RESOURCES

RESOURCES FOR DREAMS

Ann Spangler, *Dreams and Miracles* (Grand Rapids: Zondervan, 1997).

John Sanford, *Dreams and Healing: A Succinct and Lively Interpretation of Dreams* (New York: Paulist Press, 1978).

Herman Riffel, *Your Dreams: God's Neglected Gifts* (Lincoln: Chosen, 1981).

RESOURCES FOR PRAYER

Richard Foster, *Prayer: Finding the Heart's True Home* (San Francisco: HarperCollins, 1992).

James Melvin Washington, ed., *Conversations with God: Two Centuries of Prayers by African Americans* (New York: HarperPerenniel, 1994).

Duane W. H. Arnold, comp., *Prayers of the Martyrs* (Grand Rapids: Zondervan, 1991).

The Book of Common Prayer (New York: Oxford Press, 1990).

David Redding, *The Prayers I Love* (Delaware, Ohio: Starborne House, 1999).

RESOURCES FOR VESPERS

Evelyn Bence, *Spiritual Moments with the Great Hymns* (Grand Rapids: Zondervan, 1997).

Patrick Kavanaugh, *Spiritual Moments with the Great Composers* (Grand Rapids: Zondervan, 1996).

Kenneth Osbeck, *101 Hymn Stories* (Grand Rapids: Kregel, 1982).

The Cyber Hymnal, http://www.tch.simplenet.com.

RESOURCES FOR PSALMS

Philip Keller, *A Shepherd Looks at Psalm Twenty-Three* (Grand Rapids: Zondervan, 1970).

C. S. Lewis, *Reflections on the Psalms* (New York: Harcourt Brace, 1964).

Eugene H. Peterson, *Answering God: The Psalms as Tools for Prayer* (San Francisco: HarperCollins, 1991).

Leslie F. Brandt, *Psalms/Now* (St. Louis: Concordia, 1996).

Kathleen Norris, *The Psalms with Commentary* (New York: Riverhead, 1997).

John Dillenberger, *Martin Luther: Selections from His Writings* (New York: Anchor, 1962).

Maxie Dunham, *Living the Psalms: A Confidence for All Seasons* (Nashville: Upper Room, 1990).

Brent D. Earles, *Psalms for Graduates* (Grand Rapids: Baker, 1984).

James D. Capozzi, *Beside Quiet Waters: Reflections on the Psalms for Everyday Life* (New York: Continuum Press, 1999).

RESOURCES FOR POETRY

Luci Shaw, *Polishing the Petoskey Stone* (Wheaton, Ill.: Harold Shaw, 1990).

Madeleine L'Engle, *A Cry Like a Bell* (Wheaton, Ill.: Harold Shaw, 1987).

William Blake, *Poems* (New York: Albert Knopf, 1994).

Gretchen Josephson, *Bus Girl* (Cambridge: Brookline, 1997).

Resources for Stories

Leighton Ford, *The Power of Story: Rediscovering the Oldest, Most Natural Way to Reach People for Christ* (Colorado Springs: NavPress, 1994).

William R. White, *Speaking in Stories: Resources for Christian Storytellers* (Minneapolis: Augsburg Press, 1997).

William R. White, *Stories for the Gatherings: A Treasury for Christian Storytellers* (Minneapolis: Augsburg Press, 1997).

William R. White, *Stories for the Journey: A Sourcebook for Christian Storytellers* (Minneapolis: Augburg Press, 1988).

Isaac Bashinov Singer, *Stories for Children* (New York: Farrar, Straus & Giroux, 1984).

RESOURCES FOR CANTICLES

The Book of Common Prayer (New York: Oxford Univ. Press, 1990).

The United Methodist Hymnal (Nashville: United Methodist Publishing House, 1989).

Patrick Kavanaugh, *The Spiritual Lives of Great Composers* (Nashville: Sparrow, 1992).

OTHER BOOKS SUITABLE FOR NIGHTTIME READING

Robert Hudson & Shelley Townsend-Hudson, *Companions for the Soul: A Yearlong Journey of Miracles, Prayers, and Epiphanies* (Grand Rapids: Zondervan, 1995).

Lyn Cryderman, *Glory Land: A Memoir of a Lifetime in Church* (Grand Rapids: Zondervan, 1999).

Walter Wangerin Jr., *Little Lamb, Who Made Thee?* (Grand Rapids: Zondervan, 1994).

Les and Leslie Parrott, *Like a Kiss on the Lips: Meditations on Proverbs for Couples* (Grand Rapids: Zondervan, 1997).

Lucinda Secrest McDowell, *Quilts from Heaven: Finding Parables in the Patchwork of Life* (Nashville: Broadman & Holman, 1999).

David Redding, *A Rose Will Grow Anywhere: Renewing Your Confidence That God Works All Things Together for Good* (Nashville: Broadman & Holman, 1996).

Henri Nouwen, *Genesee Diary* (Garden City: Image, 1981).

Kathleen Norris, *Cloister Walk* (New York: Riverhead, 1996).

Bitsy Ayres Rubsamen, *Gentle Rain: Reflections on the Mercy of God* (Nashville: Broadman & Holman, 1998).

Linda deVries, *Spiritual Nightlights: Meditations for the Middle of the Night* (Wheaton, Ill.: Harold Shaw, 1997).

ACKNOWLEDGMENTS

Quotations from the Bible include the King James Version (KJV); the New Revised Standard Version (NRSV), © 1990 by the National Council of Churches of Christ in the United States of America; the Revised Standard Version (RSV), © 1946, 1952, 1971 by the Division of Christian Education of the National Council of Churches of Christ in the United States of America; the New International Version (NIV), © 1973, 1978, 1984 by International Bible Society; the Jerusalem Bible (JB), © 1966, 1967 and 1968 by Dartman, Longman & Todd, Ltd. and Doubleday & Co., Inc.; J. B. Phillips (JBP), © 1947, 1952, 1955, 1957 as *The Gospels* and *Letters to Young Churches* by the Macmillan Company; the New International Version Inclusive Language Edition (RNIV), edition published by Hodder & Stoughton 1996, © 1973, 1978, 1984 by the International Bible Society; *The Message* (MSG), © 1993, 1994, 1995 by Eugene H. Peterson, NavPress.

NOTES

[1]"Pieces of My Quilt" by Lucinda Secrest McDowell is reprinted with permission from *Quilts from Heaven: Finding Parables in the Patchwork of Life* (Nashville: Broadman & Holman, 1999), xiii.

[2]Gretchen Josephson, *Bus Girl* (Cambridge: Brookline, 1997), 10.

[3]William Blake, from David V. Erdman, ed., *The Complete Prose and Poetry of William Blake* (New York: Anchor, 1988), 13–14.

[4]© 1987 by Jonathan Mark Music and Birdwing Music. All rights reserved. Used by permission.

[5]Mary Taylor Previte, *Hungry Ghosts* (Grand Rapids: Zondervan, 1994), 34.

[6]Maxie Dunham, *Living the Psalms: A Confidence for All Seasons* (Nashville: Upper Room, 1990), 25–26.

[7]From Act V of Joost van den Vondel's *Lucifer,* translated by Leonard Charles van Noppen (1898).

[8]Diane M. Komp, "A Window to Heaven" in *Images of Grace: A Pediatrician's Trilogy of Faith, Hope, and Love* (Grand Rapids: Zondervan, 1996), 61.

[9]Patricia Jones-Jackson, *When Roots Die: Endangered Traditions on the Sea Islands* (Athens: Univ. of Georgia Press, 1987), 82–87. Reprinted with permission.

[10]© 1988 People of Destiny International (Administered by Copycare USA c/o The Copyright Company, Nashville, Tenn.). All rights reserved. International copyright secured. Used by permission.

[11]Kathleen Norris, *The Psalms with Commentary* (New York: Riverhead, 1997), xii–xiii.

[12]"Circles" by Luci Shaw is reprinted with permission from *Polishing the Petoskey Stone* (Wheaton, Ill.: Harold Shaw, 1990), 48.

We want to hear from you. Please send your comments about this book to us in care of the address below. Thank you.

ZondervanPublishingHouse
Grand Rapids, Michigan 49530
http://www.zondervan.com

[13]"Let Evening Come" © 1996 by the Estate of Jane Kenyon. Reprinted from *Otherwise: New & Selected Poems* with the permission of Graywolf Press, Saint Paul, Minnesota.

[14]Aleksandr Solzhenitsyn, "A World Split Apart," in Kelly Monroe, ed., *Finding God at Harvard: Spiritual Journeys of Thinking Christians* (Grand Rapids: Zondervan, 1996).

[15]Reprinted with permission from *The Prayers I Love* (Delaware, Ohio: Starborne House, 1999). © 1978, 1999 by David Redding. First printed in *Vogue*, January 1971.

[16]Kathy Coffey, "The Other Grandmother," in *Hidden Women of the Gospels* (New York: Crossroads, 1996), 26. Reprinted with permission.

We want to hear from you. Please send your comments about this book to us in care of the address below. Thank you.

ZondervanPublishingHouse
Grand Rapids, Michigan 49530
http://www.zondervan.com